Inspiring Innovation

How to Create the Magic of a

Culture of Continuous Innovation

By Lisa Kent

> *To fan the flames of innovation we must first nurture the sparks in our imaginations.*
>
> *- Unknown*

Table of Contents

Inspiring Innovation

Preface

Ever since I can remember, I was fascinated by magic. The mysterious power of witchcraft and sorcery intrigued me. While most little girls liked the princesses in Disney movies, I always gravitated toward the sorceresses and witches whose dark spells and control of other worlds changed destinies. When I got to college, I wrote my senior thesis on witchcraft in French literature and I focused on Michelet's *La Sorcière*.

In *La Sorcière*, a woman is accused of witchcraft based on the magical powers she supposedly wields. It turns out that her magic is simply the power of healing which she is able to offer because of her deep knowledge of herbs and new ways to apply them. She is not an evil witch at all, but instead she is an innovator, someone who takes new learning and creates what appears to be magic to those who don't yet understand.

Sadly, her actions and knowledge create fear and distrust and she is punished for her innovations. As was often the case for women in medieval times, she is not allowed to leverage the power of big thinking. This is seen as dangerously rebellious, and she is punished.

For much of history, innovation – new thinking, new knowledge – was viewed as something to fear, and the title of Innovator was considered a nasty word. Luckily, for us in the twenty-first century, innovation has become a way of life on many levels and is now accepted as a positive concept.

Harnessing the magic of innovation is still, today, one of my greatest joys. Figuring out ways to leverage a new technology, or an old one, to make magic for a consumer, a surgeon, a patient – that's innovation at its best.

Recently, a business magazine talked about how consumers today, continue to demand magic from the products that they buy. As an example, the article outlined how there were many mp3 music players before the iPod but Apple brought its own brand of magic to the product and ended up exploding the market.

The magic of innovation is truly what makes good companies great. Inspiring innovation in our teams and in our companies is the main path to growth. The chapters of this book are designed to help us spark that magic and remember that INNOVATOR is not a dirty word.

I have spent a good portion of my adult life working to inspire innovation among others and innovate for my clients, my brands, and many partners. Over time, I have learned a wealth of short cuts, brain tricks, and cultural approaches and have gained new wisdom that helps me drive successful innovation and growth.

Equally important, I have had the chance to learn from some of the masters – those for whom big thinking appears to come naturally. I have watched great leaders nurture an innovative and entrepreneurial spirit in others – often an indomitable one that survives even in times of daunting challenge and uncertainty.

So, I came to the conclusion that it would be beneficial to put these ideas on paper to share with my students, colleagues and friends. Even better, I realized I could ask all those experts who had been so instrumental in my life and in creating my road to innovation, what wisdom would they want to share and why? They shared generously – another facet of strong innovators.

The pages of this short book are designed to help anyone inspire and drive breakthrough ideation and create a culture of continuous innovation in their own organizations. I hope you find the stories on innovation enlightening, valuable and as magical as I do.

Section One

Innovation Interpreted

Chapter One

A Brief History of Innovation

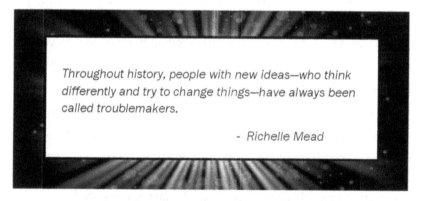

> Throughout history, people with new ideas—who think differently and try to change things—have always been called troublemakers.
>
> - Richelle Mead

In the twenty-first century, innovation is something that is celebrated and sought after by individuals and companies alike. Innovations in technology, education and medicine have vastly changed how our society thrives and interacts. However, innovation was not always seen as something positive, the way it is seen today.

To truly understand the concept of innovation, it helps to go back and look at how we got to where we are today. We need to look back in order to leap forward. So, let's take a brief tour through some of the most important innovations in human history.

Inspiring Innovation

Ancient History

If we consider the very beginning of recorded history, we see three innovations that really changed the course of human history forever – the advent of fire, the creation of language, and the evolution of the concept of barter.

In the mindset of the average Stone Age human, life was all about staying one step ahead of any large, meat-eating predator and finding enough nuts and berries to sustain life. Then one day, the concept of fire was introduced. Maybe someone struck two chunks of flint together and a spark ignited, or maybe it was a forest fire started by lightning that got Stone Age People looking in the direction of what fire could mean for life.

We may never know exactly how fire was introduced, but archeologists can tell us that the controlled use of fire first made its appearance in the early Stone Age, thought to have been between 200,000 and 600,000 years ago. Fire allowed humans to survive in colder climates and made it possible to cook and preserve food which, in turn, made migration possible.

With tribes of humans beginning to travel and interact, this gave rise to the use of language. It became possible for humans to pass on instructions from generation to generation. The use of language provided a way for humans to speed up new inventions, where each generation was able to build on what the last one created.

So, the innovations brought about by fire, language and barter paved the way for the next set of innovative historical events that furthered the overall evolution of humans. The next innovative leaps were the advent of farming, new modes of transportation (creation of the wheel and larger boats), and the invention of written language.

Inspiring Innovation

Cradle of Civilization

History shows that the first farming of animals began around 15,000 BCE and the first domestication of plants around 10,000 BCE. This step was a critical one for the advancement of the human race, as it allowed us to go from being totally nomadic to actually being able to stay in one place and build communities.

While some historians may argue over what era and what people should be credited with being the cradle of civilization, many agree that the rise of the Sumerians in Mesopotamia appears to coincide with the innovations of the wheel, use of money and the creation of written language. The Cuneiform writing of the Sumerians is the first recorded use of a stable written language and this form of communication was used for thousands of years.

The Greeks credited the goddess Athena for providing the spark of innovation needed to create the art of agriculture, mathematics, and metal work along with all the handicrafts practiced mostly by women. While the invention of the wheel, around 3400 BCE, is not credited to Athena, it qualifies as the next big thing in human history, as it gave humans a way to travel quickly on land.

The concept of ship building made an appearance around 4,000 BCE, when the ancient Egyptians began making wooden sailboards, followed by the Phoenicians and Greeks who went on to create large sailing ships. Sailing was the first form of transport that made it possible for commerce to happen between different parts of the world on a regular basis and it set the stage for a myriad of other discoveries as well.

The ability to travel quickly on land and sea then led to humans beginning trade goods and services from settlement to settlement, and the cradle of civilization was expanded. Since their homeland was basically devoid of timber, stone and minerals, the Sumerians were forced to develop trade routes in order to obtain these items.

Inspiring Innovation

The use of the sixty-second minute and the sixty-minute hour can be traced back to Mesopotamia, as well as the mathematical decimal system. Quantification of time and numbers began to give us, even back then, hurdles to beat and an understanding of real improvements.

The bottom line is that innovation has always been at the forefront of advancements in human civilization. However, the concept of innovation turned into a vastly negative one with the onset of the Dark and Middle Ages.

Innovation of Intellectual Thought

Today, innovation is spontaneously understood as technological innovation because of its contribution to economic progress in the past 200 years. However, for the previous 2,500 years, innovation had not been interpreted as positive progress.

Innovation was defined as a challenge to the status quo or a rejection of established ideas in philosophy, religion, politics and social affairs. In short, innovation in this era was seen as a vice, not a virtue, and in some cases, was used as an accusation, not a compliment.

From its advent in ancient Greece, the concept of innovation has political connotations. An innovator was introducing change into the established order and was seen as subversive or revolutionary.

While the writings of Socrates, Plato and Aristotle form the basis of current Western thinking, in their day they were innovators who were often viewed as subversives. Plato was known as a playboy from a wealthy, connected Athenian family until he met a man named Socrates. Socrates taught him that the surest path to wisdom was rational contemplation, and that being a lover of wisdom, or philosopher, was his highest form of life.

Socrates was a philosopher in ancient Athens, one who challenged the status quo by being critical of the young democracy, pointing

10

out the pitfalls and problems present in everyday life. He proposed new ways of looking at things, and his critical assessment of political life put him at odds with the ruling parties who were in no mood to be challenged after a crushing defeat at the hands of the Spartans and the loss of over twenty-five percent of the population to typhoid.

The establishment at that time did not appreciate Socrates' innovative commentary and he was arrested. The accusations against Socrates were very vague – he was accused of impiety by worshipping new gods and of corrupting the young. In actual fact, it is speculated that he was brought to trial because of his association with many outspoken aristocrats, who were all critical of democracy.

In an ironic twist, it was the new, innovative way of litigating that was the ultimate downfall of Socrates. He was tried before a jury and found guilty. Socrates went on to pay the ultimate price of an innovator – the jury voted again and he was sentenced to death by drinking poison hemlock.

Plato picked up Socrates' innovation of thought and he taught his students that most of us want to be part of something higher, something that unites everything into a single harmonious whole. There is no other road to happiness, he said, either for society or the individual, then to want to crawl out of the cave of darkness and ignorance, and walk in the light of truth.

Plato's most well-known student was Aristotle, from a family of physicians, who learned early on the value of hands-on experience and the power of observation. "Facts are the starting point of all knowledge," he wrote. So, instead of accepting Plato's view of the world, Aristotle suggested our best path to knowledge came from logical, methodical discovery. We'll talk more about this in future chapters because discovering new ideas often comes from reexamining the old ones and carefully assessing the facts we know now.

Inspiring Innovation

Historian, Arthur Herman, contends that Plato and Aristotle had vastly different views about the world, and that the various followers and interpreters of each thinker, throughout the ages, shaped the course of Western civilization. According to Herman, Plato views "the world through the eyes of the artist and religious mystic", using intuition and ideals to understand the workings of the world. Aristotle "observes reality through the... eyes of science," using reason and logic as guides.

So, while Aristotle would ask "how does it work?" Plato's question would be "why does it exist as all?" If Plato asked, "what do you want your world to be?" Aristotle would counter with "how do you fit into the world that already exists?" While these two different philosophers provided two different world views, it formed one great debate.

Aristotle espoused the theory that the light of truth is found here in the material world, and our job is to understand and find our place in the world at large. As the father of Western science (he wrote the first books on every field from biology and physics to astronomy and psychology) as well as technology, he was the paragon of logical linear thinking. On the other hand, Plato's belief in the value of intuitive leaps of imagination forms the other end of the spectrum.

The whole history of innovation and advancement of Western civilization has been a giant struggle between these two ways of seeing the world. Even within each individual, there is tension between our inner Plato and inner Aristotle when our material and logical halves argue with our spiritual and imaginative halves.

The ultimate irony, from my point of view, is that for innovation to happen we need both halves of this ideological equation. Both logic and imagination are essential to the inspiration of true innovation.

Inspiring Innovation

Innovation as Heresy

From a religious standpoint, the term innovator was also synonymous with the word heretic. The book of Common Prayer in Fourteenth Century England told parishioners not to "meddle with the folly of innovations and new fangledness." In later years, the Church of England printed lists of forbidden innovations.

While many people fled to the New World to escape religious persecution and to establish religious freedom, for the most part this simply meant that each organization wanted to be able to impose their own rules and their own truth. So, often they went from being innovators of thought, to being the keepers of the rules.

When the Puritans arrived in America, they were then free to worship as they saw fit. They established their own rules, and anyone who did something differently was labeled a heretic, or worse yet, a witch.

From the 1300's through the 1600's there were hundreds of women in Europe who were accused of witchcraft and either imprisoned or killed. When this hysteria began to wind down in Europe, it jumped the Atlantic and showed up in Salem, Massachusetts in 1692.

Many strong and creative women were accused of witchcraft simply because they were different, or had special gifts such as the power of healing. They may also have been talking about ideas that were not part of accepted rules. This innovation scared the public. Over 200 women were accused of witchcraft during the Salem trials, and 20 of them were actually put to death. Eventually, the Colony admitted that this had been done on a wave of paranoia and actually compensated the families of the victims.

Innovation of Political Thought

On the political front, the Monarchists of the seventeenth and eighteenth centuries accused the Republicans of being innovators. For centuries, the Monarchists had ruled Europe and had taken it for granted that their rule would continue to be unchallenged. However, with the Reformation happening on the religious front and democracy raising its head, the way had to be cleared for innovation in politics.

It was only after the revolutions in France and America that the tide began to turn and the concept of innovation began to have a positive meaning. As politics began to be reshaped by new ideas and revolutionary thinking, this spurred on other innovations, from manufacturing to how food was produced.

From the nineteenth century forward, a new vocabulary began to emerge surrounding innovation. It was now defined as originality of thought or combining old ideas in a new way, and this led to a new type of revolution in business.

Innovation in Manufacturing

The steam engine invented by Thomas Newcomen in 1712 or maybe even earlier by Thomas Savery, nobody knows for sure, was a historical turning point for innovation. Steam power catapulted sea travel into another dimension and when it evolved into the internal combustion engine in the mid 1800's, it was a game changer for manufacturing and communications.

There were many people participating in the new age of technological advancement. After the engine, came the light bulb, first created by English scientist Humphry Davy. (Doing research for this book I learned that, no, Thomas Edison did not invent the light bulb – he simply invented a filament that would burn for 1,500 hours instead of a few minutes.)

The telegraph, the electromagnet, the telephone, the vacuum tube, semiconductors – this is only a very short list of all the innovations that happened in the 1800's that spring-boarded us ahead in terms of manufacturing, communications and society at large.

While progress continued through the early part of the 1900's, it was after World War II that innovations such as transistors, integrated circuits, the internet, microprocessors and mobile/smart phones completely altered the reality of our world.

Innovation of the Future

Innovation is a critical part of civilization and the advancement of the human race. It is the only way for society and business to thrive and grow. Adapt proactively or suffer the consequences.

However, in many companies, organizations and governmental bodies today there is still a sense that innovators are heretics. Innovation and challenging the status quo is often not welcomed. Breaking down barriers is too rarely rewarded and thus too rarely occurs. This has to change.

In the next few chapters I have laid out what I have found to be the best way to approach growing a culture of innovation within a company or organization. Now that the history is covered, we can focus on the future.

Take Away Tips

- Look backward at history to leap forward toward progress.
- Fight the tendency to view innovators or disruptors as heretics and welcome the thinking instead.
- Innovation is a critical part of civilization and the advancement of the human race.

Chapter Two

A Fine Blend of Chaos and Discipline

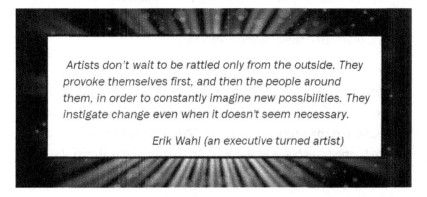

> *Artists don't wait to be rattled only from the outside. They provoke themselves first, and then the people around them, in order to constantly imagine new possibilities. They instigate change even when it doesn't seem necessary.*
>
> *Erik Wahl (an executive turned artist)*

The first rule of innovation is that there is no first rule. Innovative chaos is trying many things, being open to anything and, in essence, throwing a lot of things against the wall to see what sticks. Or, putting it another way: don't put edges on it, just get the ideas out on the table and then begin to sort them.

As a leading player in the arena of innovation, Google is willing to invest in chaos. They created a culture where their people can have a safe platform to try and fail until they get to a marketable innovation.

Also high on the list of innovation priorities within Google is the concept that innovation can come from anywhere, from a personal assistant to the Chairman of the Board. For example, a medical doctor, who was employed to look after the health of Google's staff, came forward with a unique observation and argued with great persuasion that the company had a moral obligation to help redirect people searching the topic of how to commit suicide.

In response to his challenge, Google adjusted the algorithms of their search engine so that the top response was always the toll-free phone number for the National Suicide Prevention Hotline – call volume went up by almost 10 percent soon after.

As a way of tapping into the chaos theory of innovation, Google also supports their twenty percent rule. While it is necessary to have defined job roles with specific deliverables, the company provides for each of their employees to spend twenty percent of their time working on a project that they are passionate about, even if it is not directly related to their defined job role.

Chaos is often the first step in ideation, it is the storming that happens first. Given a specific challenge, I often begin with many different people with a variety of backgrounds, some of whom have no relation to the problem at hand. They are then briefed on what we are trying to achieve and it is up to them to help storm the ideas and try to help us solve it.

Thought Leaders on Chaos

In their book The Chaos Imperative: How Chance and Disruption Increase Innovation Effectiveness and Success, Ori Brafman and Judah Pollack argue that we should proactively seek to avoid the tyranny of structure in order to inspire creativity and fuel business growth. They show that some of the most disruptive innovations happened during times of need and in an environment of chaos. "There is a paradox at the heart of chaos," the authors maintain. "For all the destructive power of the chaos, [for example], unleashed by the Black Plague [in Europe], it turned out to be the crucible in which the modern Western world was forged... It may seem magical and bizarre that the Renaissance came about so quickly after the plague." However, when we look back, it happens again and again throughout history and within organizations.

In the present day, Brafman and Pollack state that "to the surprise of neuroscientists, there appears to be a whole area of the brain that flourishes when we let a bit of chaos into our lives. It's what allows us to solve problems in a novel way."

Chaos can be uncomfortable, especially in the ordered world of business. Jason Fried, CEO of 37signals, announced one day that the entire company would take a month off from non-essential assigned work to see what the teams could do with no structured schedule whatsoever. It was an experiment, a test of sorts.

At first employees were uncomfortable, they were unsure what to do with such a long stretch of uninterrupted time with no imposed structure. But soon after, Fried said, people started to come up with amazing ideas: "a new way to sell one of our products, a better way to keep our customers informed, a fresh take on surprising customers with better service, and a better way to introduce new employees to the rest of the company. I was blown away by the creativity, polish, and execution."

Author Erik Wahl talks about Honda and its founder Soichiro Honda in *Unthink: Rediscover Your Creative Genius*. Wahl explains that Honda's approach of purposeful provocation was used to inspire change and create progress.

Honda experienced numerous crises and setbacks in its early years, everything from a factory being destroyed by fire, to wartime rationing. "After a while Honda began to note how each crisis improved the eventual outcome," says Wahl. "Ironically, the trials often sharpened his workers and left his company with better results than if everything had gone as scripted. For example, it took a steel shortage for him to discover that aluminum not only made lighter engine blocks but also dissipated heat better. A design failure that seemed catastrophic turned out to be the doorway to a landmark innovation."

Sony's chairman, Akio Morita, perpetuated the Sony free spirit through a series of unusual policies: hiring brilliant people with non-traditional skills for high management positions (such as an opera singer), and promoting young people over experienced personnel. Both of these practices were perceived as chaotic, out of the norm of understood management theory, but they brought results.

The history of technology is littered with the chaos of accidents, mishaps, and chance meetings that created a path to success, even though the ideas began in chaos. Leo Baekelund was looking for a synthetic shellac when he found Bakelite which was the inception of the modern plastics industry. At Syntex, researchers were looking for something else entirely when they created 19-norprogesterone, the precursor to the active ingredient in half of all contraceptive pills.

And, of course, one of the most famous chaos-to-success stories came out of industry giant 3M, where a failed attempt at making an adhesive led to the million-dollar industry we now know as Post-It® notes. Such accidents are involved in many major technological advances. However, in order to reach success, these organizations must be ready to deal with chaos, and know how to capitalize on it quickly to turn it into a marketable innovation.

Ori Brafman, who is also the author of, *The Chaos Imperative: How Chance and Disruption Increase Innovation, Effectiveness, and Success* makes the point that "In times of uncertainty, the temptation is to create more structure and order. Because that feels safe and predictable. However, in times of uncertainty you also

need a lot of innovation the way to foster innovation is by bringing organized chaos into the system."

From Chaos to Discipline

Celebrating and leaning into a chaotic moment in a marketplace, an industry or a product's lifecycle works. Yet, while chaos is a key ingredient in creating innovation, discipline and order must be part of the mix as well. It is important to follow a prescribed process in an allotted timeframe with defined deliverables, in order to create innovation that grows a business or organization.

We have created a proven program for our clients called the Luminations Lightning Strike®, which is our hyper-effective brainstorming process that allows us to help our clients create the magic of continuous innovation. It is a way for us to work from within our client's organization to help them create innovation around a specific product or service, or simply to help them create a culture of innovation.

As part of our Lightning Strike® process, we have a very disciplined first phase called Discovery. Discovery leads to a brief and then, ultimately, the ideas.

Leveraging Different Types of Brainstorming

Last year, I had the opportunity to facilitate and plan two different brainstorming sessions that leveraged very disparate entities. Each project involved a relatively staid, disciplined healthcare company that innovates often but uses a rigorous approach, and a division of Google (known for its wild-ass innovative thinking).

One of the partnerships was in life sciences, with Google's Verily. The other one was in advertising with Google's catalyst advertising business development team. In both cases, the healthcare companies were partnering with Google to bring new ideas, products or services to life. In both cases, the combination of skills and the incredibly different approaches to innovation each company represented led to some really inspired thinking.

As the two innovation pathways collided, brilliant sparks of magic began to fly.

The planning and preparation for the sessions began to unveil the companies' very different approaches as the brainstorm objectives and logistics unfolded. One side of the brainstorm team was eager to conduct pre-meetings with me, planning every aspect of our objectives and deliverables. I found this practice reassuring, as I like to exceed clients' expectations and cannot do that unless I know what they are.

On the Google side, they gleefully allocated a team of thinkers and innovators to the project. These folks agreed to show up for the session, but were not readily available for any planning meetings. I found them to be as insightful and talented as the healthcare clients when I could connect with them, but very little if anything was ever documented.

Our goals, in both cases, were lofty: Ideate and identify disruptive and breakthrough approaches to address a critical business challenge or opportunity. For one of the sessions, we held the team meeting in the large medical company's beautifully appointed conference room. It was covered in teak wood and was known to be state of the art. The doors were closed in the hushed hallways for maximum confidentiality.

While the place was wonderful, it did not necessarily inspire optimal breakthrough thinking. The Luminations team had to work hard to create an environment that fostered creativity and fun. While not insurmountable, it required gorgeous posters, creative collages, toys, crayons and bubble gum to pull some magic into the situation.

For the other session, we booked a room at Google's NYC headquarters. Security in the building was tight but after that, the journey was magical. To get to this room, we had to walk past a wall of grasses, a winter-ski-lodge-themed micro kitchen (which was actually huge) and the room itself was named for a seasonal fun activity. We were encouraged to help ourselves to their plethora of food, including 5 types of coffees each brewed in a different vessel, but warned that Googlers could pop into any meeting they liked so we might have surprise guests.

The freethinking and brainstorming began way before we got into our conference room. Our breakout room had no tables, just large foam cushions we could sit on, climb on, or I guess – if I was not an engaging facilitator – sleep on. Fortunately, nobody dozed. We posted our ideas on colorful clings and put them up on the glass walls, and a cascade of ideas flowed.

As I worked to keep us moving through our many fast-paced exercises, even the language and questions from both teams was very different. Safety, focus on truly understanding the customer came from one side and breaking through barriers, re-imagining a category that customers couldn't possibly articulate came from others.

Where prototypes were involved, Google just built, tested, optimized and did it again. Other companies began instead with concepts, drawings, maybe even 3D animations. The idea of a fully operational prototype that would likely be discarded was crazy. Or was it? High tech and software companies usually build something that mostly works, they launch it and fix the bugs as they go.

In healthcare, partly due to regulation but also because this is just how it's always been done, claims are clinically proven before they are uttered and prototypes come much later in the process. To really innovate, to re-imagine the way we had to in both of these categories, we actually needed earlier prototypes AND substantial claims. We needed to understand deep customer or consumer insights AND give them what they didn't even know to ask for – this hybrid pathway to innovation brought great early results.

Inspiring Innovation

Our list of priority ideas was long and rich. By recognizing the divergent styles and designing exercises that leveraged both, the two groups built on each other's strengths and helped break down each other's barriers. The combination, better yet, collision of chaos with control, risk with care, and brilliant minds on both sides illustrated that this is the future of innovation. I was very happy to be a part of it.

Striking the Balance

Attempting to innovate without any boundaries could lead to ineffective results. However, the application of too many bureaucratic rules means that innovation is strangled. In an article in the magazine *Fast Company*, a story is published outlining how the company Lego® "has grown into nothing less than the Apple of toys, a profit-generating, design-driven miracle built around premium, intuitive, highly covetable hardware of which fans can't get enough."

Several years ago, fueled in part by *The Lego Movie*'s massive popularity, the privately-held company briefly surged ahead of rival Mattel® to become the biggest toy manufacturer in the world. It was a remarkable achievement; particularly considering that Mattel® makes a huge range of products while Lego® mostly sticks to variations on a single toy.

Every year, Lego's Future Lab team meets in Spain. This is the Danish toy giant's secretive and highly ambitious R&D team, charged with inventing entirely new, technologically-enhanced play experiences for kids all over the world. They play, they learn from Lego® masters, they swim, and eventually they present business recommendations. Like Google, they prototype quickly and fully expect many failures. Through a balance of chaos and discipline, this elite team continues to innovate, keeping the Lego Group at the forefront of the toy innovators.

Take Away Tips

- Striking a balance between discipline and chaos often yields the most compelling innovation.
- Allow free thinking and unfocused time to generate a wide array of ideas.
- Use a deliberate process to set priorities and prototype.

Inspiring Innovation

Section Two

Innovation Inspired

Chapter Three

Environmental Elements

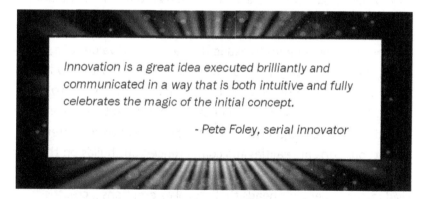

> *Innovation is a great idea executed brilliantly and communicated in a way that is both intuitive and fully celebrates the magic of the initial concept.*
>
> *- Pete Foley, serial innovator*

Creating the Right Environment for Innovation

The right environment for Innovation consists of five important factors:

1) A clear vision.
2) The right blend of chaos and discipline.
3) An engaging physical environment.
4) Cutting edge technology and tools to help innovate remotely and in person.
5) Keeping the consumer close.

A Compelling Vision

While both chaos and discipline are important elements in creating a culture of continuous innovation, we must provide a clear vision and the right environment as well. There has to be a defined destination. What is the organization trying to achieve? What is the ultimate vision for a particular team or product? Where do they see themselves in the future?

When planning a vacation, we first, pick a destination. Then it becomes possible to begin selecting the other variables such as mode of transportation, places to stay, things to do – it all begins to fall into place with a vision of the destination.

At a higher level, for a business or an organization, a vision is a collected set of ideas that describe what the future should look like – the vision should provide a high bar, so high that our imaginations have to grapple with the concept.

A vision statement needs to exude the passion and values of a team, company, or organization. It should be short, just a few lines, clear, and written in the present tense. It looks 5-10 years into the future but is written as if we could experience it right now. We should be able to imagine it coming to life. A great vision statement reflects our current realities and competencies but builds on them. Erica Olson states, and I agree, that a vision statement "creates a vivid image in people's heads that provokes emotions... creates enthusiasm and gives a longer sense of purpose".

Once there is a clear destination, then it is time to look at how the team comes together and what environment is needed to germinate the magic of innovation.

The Intersection of Innovation and Physical Space

Two Finnish professors, Kaisa Oksanen and Pirjo Ståhle, investigated the intersection of physical space and innovation and came up with some interesting findings which they documented in the *Journal of Knowledge Management.*

All of their research reinforced the concept of a relationship between the physical space and the ability for humans to be their best at the art of innovation. They identified five specific characteristics that make for the best innovative spaces: collaboration-enabling, modifiability, smartness, value-reflecting, and attractiveness.

> *Collaboration-enabling – A space that enables collaboration was found to be critical as both innovation and creativity are widely acknowledged as collaborative processes, and all spaces examined reinforced that innovation is a social process. Collaboration-enabling spaces are those that motivate and afford people the opportunity to share knowledge and experiences, for example through office layouts where community members work alongside one another rather than in separate rooms.*

> *Modifiability – Just as innovation requires flexible thinking, innovative spaces require flexible design. This includes options to change lighting, seating, and even rooms within a space, as well as the ability to use the same space for very different purposes. Learning and research spaces examined in this study were found to be built to allow for users to engage in a wide variety of activities and collaborate with others in novel ways while studying/working. Varied, flexible spaces allow for those of diverse backgrounds and interests to converge in a single place and interact through cross-functional work and learning groups.*

> *Smartness – Largely focused on technology, smart spaces are those that are enabled for co-operation of smart objects and systems and for ubiquitous interaction with different users. Technology is and will increasingly be used to connect*

and collaborate with team members we may not have had access to otherwise.

Value-reflecting – In the research, this characteristic was well-summarized by an interviewee: "What do the best companies have in common spatially? Their spaces provide a message or a story about the organization. Space is full of symbols, and, if utilized wisely – for example, through art – the space can have wide psychosocial impacts on their users." The values of innovation include openness, sustainability and collaboration, and it was found that innovative spaces mirror these values.

Attractiveness – A study respondent stated that, "Interesting space attracts interesting people." Attractive spaces are – at minimum – safe and comforting. However, attractive can also mean ergonomics and interior design, as well as its surrounding location.

Implications

These researchers have produced a study that suggests that the leaders of organizations need to make strategic decisions about what environment they provide for where work gets done. Globally, we are seeing a change in the business cubical model and companies are choosing to create transformational spaces that allow for people to connect, share ideas and communicate on every level.

Will having a space with all of these characteristics guarantee innovation and creativity? Not necessarily – it still depends on having the right people to populate the ideal work environment.

While physical space makes a difference, in 2017, a significant amount of our innovation work, and our clients' is done virtually. Creating the right virtual environment can be even more valuable than attractive office space. Enabling online collaboration through open dialogue and technology tools, building on each other's ideas and refining together, and creating clear communication processes are all essential.

This is Luminations' modus operandi as all of our innovators are scattered around the globe. One client, Clorox®, also conducts virtual innovation exceptionally. They are not afraid to invest in the technology that facilitates it and reward leaders who incentivize it. As a result, these virtual collaborations generate strong, measurable innovation.

Shining Example, guess who?

Google, one of my favorite examples, manages its virtual connections and physical environment well. Their unique approach includes unlimited food and coffee, unusual work spaces, sleep/rest areas, open planning for offices and a Chief Happiness Officer whose main goal is to listen to staff and determine what they need to continue to be happy.

Google strategically builds their offices near locations that contain access to public transport and great living spaces. The internal décor is always colorful and fun, and offices exude a sense of play, including doors disguised as bookshelves that lead to secret reading nooks. Employees can design their own desks from oversized Tinker-Toy® like components and scribbling on the walls in encouraged. Amazon, who recently announced it was seeking bids for a second headquarters location, espouses a similar philosophy.

By providing this open, creative and non-structured environment, Google gives its people tacit permission to innovate and feel fully-supported. They can stay focused on creative thinking without the distraction of having to worry about where to get lunch, or if they have time to run errands.

While Google is reimagining how office space in constructed and used, there are other companies that have been working on innovative ways to make telecommuting work. Referring back to Clorox® they endeavor to keep people connected through software and shared whiteboards, WebEx® and Skype® that enable open dialogues and innovation. They are organized into studios instead of franchises, so they foster innovation across different disciplines.

While virtual teams can create wonderful innovations, there is still much to be said for in-person innovation across many disciplines to really create magical innovation. Johnson & Johnson, for several high profile launches, decided to bring together cross-functional partners all in one space in a desire to accelerate innovation. This was an arrangement that had proven successful in the past. It makes the relationships and the communication a priority.

Following this same line of thought, GlaxoSmithKline created an entire innovation wing where the marketing and finance team work on the floor of a shared R&D lab. A team member in Finance only had to turn around to look at the lab bench to figure out what materials he was costing out. If teams are physically together, it becomes very important to make the relationships and the communication a focus. It is necessary to make use of all the tools available to make sure the connection back to functional areas is not lost.

Mars was one of the first companies years and years ago that created an open floor plan office. At the time, it was pretty controversial and it was uncomfortable for new hires who were used to a much more traditional floor plan. Then, over the years, companies like Pfizer Consumer Health and Johnson and Johnson moved to that same kind of look and feel. There's a de factor open-door policy because there are no doors that will create barriers to communication.

It's important to note, though, that I've seen as much creativity come from an industrial warehouse setting as from the perfect office. Many of our entrepreneurial clients work in less-than-ideal settings as they invest in the early stages of their business ideas.

Creative people trump creative surroundings in almost all cases. It's great if we can find both.

Virtual Challenge

Valeant, although they have faced their share of financial challenges, had a management team on their consumer business that were big proponents of working virtually. In their skincare franchise, the head of R&D was on the West Coast and many of the other team members were scattered throughout the East Coast. Yet they still maintained an incredible pace of innovation for their skin care brand, CeraVe®. This was partly due to the leadership fostering regular and informal communication, cutting out many phases of bureaucracy that bogged people down, and enabling the time spent together virtually to be productive and results-oriented. The head of this team led in a way that embodied the kind of innovation discussed in the interviews I've conducted. She talks about the power of extreme trust, autonomy, diversity of thought, and a clear vision, and she delivered on each of these elements, making it possible for her team to create the magic of true innovation.

The challenge with using virtual tools to stay connected is that the chance encounter at the water cooler or in the hallway no longer happens – and that can be one important opportunistic way to spark innovation. As BCG redesigned its offices to foster more casual collisions, they are finding better attendance and results. Google capitalizes on this by having rooms with ping-pong tables, and a music room for jam sessions. Once the mind is relaxed from one of these leisure time activities it may wake up and the magic of innovation can then shine through.

In a virtual organization, trust is very important, because the team cannot take the time to report in detail on every step. Trusted colleagues enable innovation to happen at a faster pace. Not just people that management trust, but team members who trust each other through both a shared history of proven success and the ability to work and to play nicely together. At Luminations, much of our ideation work is done virtually. This requires a clear vision or brief, alignment on approach and unfiltered communication.

Creative Ways of Keeping the Consumer Close

While the environment contributes some, I think the most important thing to inspire innovation is ensuring closeness to the consumer.

What does this look like? Physically interacting and communicating with a target audience is often the first step. Immersing ourselves and seeing what they are seeing should be the norm. Pandora® Jewelry has a physical store in their building. Elizabeth Arden, built a spa and salon in the first-floor lobby of its headquarters. Equinox Fitness and Blink Fitness have their gyms on the same block. Ideo®'s principles of design thinking often reflect consumer empathy as a first step and this cannot occur without closeness or even immersion in a consumer, patient, or user's life.

At Johnson & Johnson, they have built a Consumer Experience Center in their consumer building to touch base with consumers on a variety of topics and to watch them use new products and react. Those are the things that help a company gain the insight when they need to innovate. This closeness puts them in a position to constantly test and learn. Those companies that make products or services where they can see and feel their consumer environment – those are the companies that get the best information to begin their innovation. Of course, the sweetest example may be Nestle, as they have a test kitchen AND a restaurant in their headquarters.

We worked with a company called Palomar Medical Technologies. They develop devices to treat and enhance skin. They have a dermatologist's office on the first floor of their main building. So as they're developing new technology for skin care they are able to see both the clinicians and patients react to it in real time

Inspiring Innovation

My mom goes to the studios of Clairol to get her hair dyed in New York City. They test new colors and new products. The stylists actually do the coloring and styling for free for the volunteer consumers. However, the consumer has to want to be a guinea pig. The testers and the stylists both offer valuable feedback throughout the development process.

No matter how wonderful the environment, success still depends on having the right minds in that environment to tap into the magic of innovation. To create an environment that inspires innovation companies and organizations must value and reward the innovators.

Take Away Tips

- The optimal environment to inspire innovation often requires:
    - A clear vision.
    - A physically attractive and flexible space for collaborative collisions.
    - All the technological tools that allow easy virtual collaboration.
    - Clear communication.
    - Standing close to the consumer.

Chapter Four

Mentorship Matters

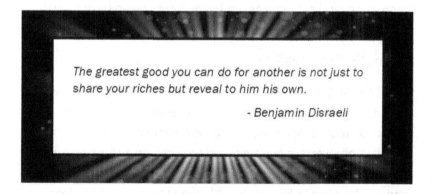

> *The greatest good you can do for another is not just to share your riches but reveal to him his own.*
>
> *- Benjamin Disraeli*

One of the most vital ingredients for creating home grown innovators is meaningful mentorship. Mentors are a lot like parents – it is all about drawing out the best in our team member or our child. I wrote an article called "What Parenthood Taught Me About Management" and some of my thoughts on the parallels are included here, too.

Both mentors and parents must possess patience, tenacity, enthusiasm, a positive attitude and the ability to know when to let go of the reins. A helicopter parent is someone who is so afraid of their child getting hurt that they hover like a helicopter and prevent the child from taking any chances. When it comes to mentoring innovation within an organization, it is very important to put the helicopter away.

My first and greatest mentors were my parents, who offered many nurturing traits including an undying confidence in abilities I didn't even know I had, a willingness to break down barriers for me, and an ability to teach me new things constantly. My dad focused on inspiring me to think bigger and to expand my horizons. My mom was a positive energy force, always cheering me on. One major aspect of a great mentor is cheerleading. Nobody can have too many cheerleaders, right?

For me, mentors made a big difference to me and my professional development. Throughout my career I was fortunate to have many mentors, several of whom agreed to be interviewed for this book, and I have shared several of these interviews in Chapter 8.

Fighting the Fear of Failure

One of the first things than mentors and leaders need to address is the fear of failure. They need to provide encouragement and support so that team members feel safe enough to think big. If an organization invests in learning, and provides an atmosphere where experimentation is encouraged and rewarded, it sets the right tone. Leaders also need to know when it's time to leave a team alone, to value those who raise their hands to do something different. A mentor needs to be able to celebrate failure and the benefits of learning from it.

No one likes to fail. However, failure brings about defining moments and important lessons that success never would. Children (and adults) can't always see this and often get discouraged. A mentor cannot shield someone from all disappointments, failures or stressful situations – they just need to be there for support to help pick up the pieces and let them know that it ok to fail, as long as they try again.

Thomas Edison is often credited with inventing the light bulb. However, history records that there are many people over time that had invented something similar to the light bulb. Instead, it seems that no one was able to figure out which material to use for the filament so that it would not burn out too quickly.

Edison and his team worked for years trying to establish what material could be used for a filament in a light bulb that would not burn out within just a few hours. Legend has it that they tried over 1,000 times with many different materials. He was once asked how it felt to have failed so many times and his response was that he did not view it as failure – he now knew 1,000 ways the light bulb would NOT work. When Edison and his team created a filament that lasted 1200 hours, it was finally deemed a success. Without all those failures the light bulb would never have become a reality. If they'd feared failure or reprimand, this team would've stopped trying, and we would still be reading by the light of a gas lamp!

Rewarding the Belly Flops

Looking at mentorship through the eyes of a parent, kids need to learn to handle difficulty in order to cope with challenges. If parents (and mentors) just reward the home runs and the perfect dives and show disappointment in the strike outs and belly flops, then kids may become afraid to take chances and try new things. It is the same for mentorship.

A leader must make it acceptable to fail or employees will never take risks. A culture that punishes mistakes squelches innovation. Being part of a cohesive team requires providing the necessary framework to reward the perfect dives as well as those risks that might turn out to be belly flops. If no one in business took risks, we'd still all be using taxicabs, not Uber.

Inspiring Innovation

Good mentors don't take themselves too seriously. If innovators and their mentors take themselves too seriously, their hearts and minds are not necessarily free enough to see the possibilities. It is important to replace paralyzing fear with laughter and acceptance. This is not to suggest that removing all fear is a good thing. A little fear, a nagging feeling in the gut or a bit of nerves, sometimes stimulates imagination. In fact, when something scares me, I know I might have stumbled onto a breakthrough. Nelson Mandela said he learned that "courage was not the absence of fear, but the triumph over it".

Mentors value diversity of thought and skills because this blend is what brings innovation to the forefront. At Luminations, we maintain engineers on each team along with our creative folks. While we may lead the blue sky thinking as marketers, I want to be sure we have the discipline of engineers thinking differently about the same problem. It is critically important to value, recruit and nurture diversity of thought and skills and see them as pivotal to solving problems. This and mentorship are two of the major themes that emerged in my interviews with innovators.

Neal Matheson, former head of R&D at J&J, Procter and Gamble, and Unilever, said in his interview that he was able to generate a lot of breakthrough innovation because he valued diversity of thought. He deliberately hired people who thought differently than he did, to challenge his thinking. I try to follow his example and surround myself with smart people who think differently than I do and who are not afraid to challenge me.

Mentoring the Mentor

While I often have the privilege of mentoring my team or even my clients, there have been many people over the course of my professional career that have shown me the way. One of the first mentors to really spark innovative thinking in me was Doug Hall, the founder of the Eureka® Ranch in Cincinnati and of the Innovation Engineering Institute.

He was a Procter and Gamble marketer from the Boston area whose colorful speech was always peppered with the words "wicked" and "awesome". He had a contagious energy and charisma that made us want to be around him.

He was an innovator and marketer, but on the side he designed games. When he left P&G he created this place where we could take our teams and go to generate new ideas: the Eureka Mansion and then later the Eureka Ranch. In the period of a couple of days, we would go from a brain dump of hundreds of ideas to a dozen completely written concepts ready to test. His process pulled out what was already in people's brains and broke down any pre-existing notions or assumptions. He fostered a boundless thinking, free-speaking collaboration. I never walked out of one of his sessions without being inspired and without generating more than the number of ideas I had hoped to generate.

Doug's method helped opened up people's minds to associative logic and to hidden connections. It happened quite often that a few days after I was at one of his sessions or at his ranch, I would come up with a big idea. The free flow of ideas didn't just stop when I was walking out of his building. Once my mind began flowing in a very productive and imaginative way, I could put things together that I hadn't put together that way before.

Doug deployed people he called "trained brains". These were people trained to think differently and to nurture this ability in others. I was lucky enough to be trained by him to do this and to go back to my company and spark innovation as if we were at the Eureka® Ranch. Because we couldn't always physically be there, we trained brains, and brought the innovation culture back to New Jersey.

That was something that I brought with me to manage the kind of innovation that I lead now. We always say that we're going to generate a lot of ideas when we're together, however, when we do a Lightning Strike® session with our clients, we send a virtual post-it note out two days after the event to remind everybody that they shouldn't ignore the ideas that flow afterward. They should write down those ideas that come to them in the shower, in the car, on the train in the next couple of days if we do out job right, many more ideas will come.

What Doug Hall inspired in me is the expectation that even the toughest challenges can be solved, when we look at them a different way with a team of smart people. From working with Doug, I also realized that innovation could be taught through imaginative and breakthrough thinking could be taught and developed, as opposed to assuming this was an innate skill. While it may be true that some people are born with a natural ability to think big, everybody, and I mean everyone, can learn to do it.

I've spoken about my J&J mentors before and Sharon D'Agostino was one of them. She had a way of making people believe in their potential and their possibilities. She instilled confidence so that we believed we could achieve something even if we'd never done it before. The bottom line was that we always wanted to give 110% when working with Sharon. We knew that her expectation was that we would always bring our best effort and ideas. This encouragement and clearly articulated expectation always made us want to dazzle her with our innovative magic. Great mentors not only offer support in challenging times, but also make us want to dazzle them. Her high hopes came from a place of believing in us, not tearing us down; pulling us up to drive our business.

Ultimately, Sharon became the head of Corporate Giving for Johnson and Johnson. She was all about going beyond the endless possibilities of building the business to the endless possibilities of healing the world. She worked to make life better for women and children around the globe. To know that the company selected her for that role was also inspiring. Many people wanted to follow her there. What better than to give away millions a year for causes that are important? She found that it's just as hard to select where to give most donations, as it is to select where to invest in innovation. She made sure funds went to organizations where they work the hardest and have the most impact. Not only did Sharon inspire the people that worked with her and the constituencies of Johnson and Johnson that trusted her to make these decisions, but she also inspired the thousands of women whose lives she touched.

When I see her interact with various organizations today, people speak to her and look at her with undying respect and gratitude. They also truly share her desire to do right because that's the expectation emanating from her. This is a prime illustration of how great mentors make us want to do our best and be our best, not out of fear but out of pride.

Mentors must be willing to stand up for their teams and break down barriers for them. Several innovator interviewees stated that they saw their role as protecting and shielding their teams. Owen Rankin, who was President of the Johnson's Baby Company when I worked for him, was a senior leader who created environments to help his team do its best. He shielded us from all the politics that could hamper our efforts. He saw his job as paving the way for us to get our job done in an effective and powerful way.

Owen was one of my first managers who really preached giving our best efforts both to work and family. He actually walked the talk. He coached his kids in soccer and made time for everybody on his team at work and expected other people to do the same: make their families a priority as well as their work and not be ashamed to say so.

Family time used to be something that we snuck away to do and didn't put on our calendars. If we left for a school play, a Halloween parade, or a child's dentist appointment, it was a risk. It was seen as a potential lack of work focus. Working for Owen, this was no longer a secret. It was part of our identity and something he wanted to cultivate as much as our professional strengths.

That was inspirational to me as a mentee and became core to my values as a mentor. It helped me see that I could foster that spirit for my team, too. My current business model offers part-timers, who may have family obligations, the opportunity to do incredible strategic work at the same time as they consult. Owen made me see that it was possible to care about family and invest in family and still deliver great business results. He expected awesome business results and guess what? People gave their best, and they were happy to do so. Like my mom has been, he was a cheerleader and he never let anything get him down.

Sharon was that way, too. Her screen saver on her computer used to be "There is always a way." I believe that there is always a way. Owen would, if there were no clear path, plow one for us. Mentors teach us new ways to succeed and open new pathways. They let us try and, often, fail before we succeeded. The good ones give us enough runway to be smart, independent professionals, and recognize the whole person. They build up confidence in new and challenging situations, whether business challenges, political challenges, or personal challenges. A good mentor will espouse the attitude that there is always a way, and stand up for and support his or her mentees. Mentors will offer freedom, but also provide a safety net.

So Happy Together

My favorite mentors have always been people with whom I want to be. I just wanted to be in their orbit. This is part of inspiring innovation, too. Creating a think-big, can-do culture also means warmth and gratitude. We want to be with these influencers and to prove them right. In essence, we need to say 'I can do it. I can think big and I deserve the confidence and affection that this leader is sending my way.'

People don't want to be around those who are negative; it is uninspiring . Nothing kills creativity more quickly than somebody stomping on an idea. Walking into a room that has palpable negative energy just shuts everyone and their creativity down. In order to inspire innovation we have to be positive. My friend and motivational speaker Joey Himelfarb hands out business cards to remind us that positivity beats negativity every day. And, at the end of the day, the magic of innovation can only happen in a positive environment.

Mentoring Mission - Building Knowledge

One of the most important things that I do to mentor my current team is to work to expand their horizons. I hope to teach them new things, and give them lots of autonomy and independence. In addition to providing them with any new knowledge and experiences I've obtained, I also ask them to do the same.

They are encouraged to take classes on any topic of their choice, every year. Some of those classes have been about digital analytics and some have been about the science of natural ingredients and some have been on personal coaching. They cover a wide range of seminars that may or may not have immediate relevance for their work today. If they think it stretches them and will enhance their thinking in any way, their only obligation is to take notes and share a summary with the rest of the team.

I take several classes or attend conferences every year. One year, I went to the Toy Fair, this year included a visit to the Firehouse Expo and a learning-filled Procter & Gamble Alumni Reunion event. I recently took a series of webinars on new digital metrics and the emerging eco system around the cannabis industry. Every year there are many learning sessions available from the Consumer Health Products Association. I personally love the learning experience and I never know where the next kernel of innovation is going to come from.

The Power of Mentors Who Support Volunteerism

Volunteering, sponsored and endorsed by a mentor, instills the value of giving back and allows another kind of experience to develop and reward talent. Some of my most influential mentors have come from my nonprofit work. At Luminations, we have our charity of choice program. Everybody is encouraged to give back to their communities or to causes that are important to them. If there is anything that is needed in that effort, they can draw on the rest of the team to help, pro bono. We might name a new program, develop fundraising collateral, or plan sponsorship packages or events. We always draw on each other's expertise and we expect to be asked to reciprocate.

Luminations currently sponsors two shelters and programs for women and children in need. One is called WomanSpace and one is called Safe&Sound. In addition to offering needed services or products to these groups, this is another important reminder to be grateful for what we have and to give to those who may not be as fortunate as we are. We often focus on women and children who are escaping abusive relationships. Their needs are great and there is so much we can do to help.

Another way that I try to mentor involves reaffirming, for my team, my complete confidence in them. They know I believe that they can tackle lots of things they may never have done before. I try to stretch them into roles that may feel uncomfortable or unfamiliar at first. Roles that they may not have otherwise considered are great opportunities. I work to support them if they are facing something they don't know how to tackle and to break down barriers with clients or partners to make it easier for them to achieve success. As with all of my endeavors, I believe I can improve as a mentor and seek frequent input and feedback.

Giving Back

A lot of being a great mentor comes from making connections. We never know where the next idea or growth trajectory is going to come from and helping to network and connect is imperative as it opens up doors and opportunities. Along with a personal connection to me comes an open invitation to leverage our virtual and physical network. Our LinkedIn user group, the LumiNATION, hosts many professional job postings and learning opportunities. Our annual client appreciation event is my favorite connection moment.

A seasoned mentor will naturally facilitate warm introductions or hand offs, not cold ones. A warm introduction means the mentor opens the dialogue, finds a commonality for their mentee, and then hands off the conversation or connection.

Just as important as fostering introductions and networking is being a good listener. A good listener is a nonjudgmental listener, someone who offers guidance or just listens when the time is appropriate. This is another parallel with good parenting, by the way.

Improved listening skills are one of the best takeaways I learned in one of my volunteer roles, as an EMT. It's often in listening to the patient that we figure out what's really going on. Or, if the patient is unconscious or too young to speak, it means listening carefully to their family or witnesses. I think I've gotten much better at that over time. Listening for clues, listening for soft ideas, but not for judgment. As a mentor, this skill is as pivotal as offering advice.

Mentoring Collaboration on the way to Innovation

Many people think of Thomas Edison as the lone inventor, when in fact most of his inventions were the results of collaborations with a large team of people. Sarah Miller Caldicott is Edison's grandniece and she recently published a book entitled *Midnight Lunch* where she talks about how collaboration powers innovation.

When we look around our modern world we can trace so many industries today back to Thomas Edison: movies, recorded sound, storage batteries and electrical power just to name a few. His lifetime bridged two centuries; his life's work is truly astounding and is a testament to the magic of innovation.

The title of the book *Midnight Lunch* comes from the affectionate term that Edison's employees, at his Menlo Park lab, gave to his practice of staying late to run experiments and then serving a team dinner. He would often go home around 5 pm to have dinner with his family and then return to the lab around 7 pm to see how various experiments were faring. He would speak to team members, encourage them to share insights with each other and then around 9 pm he would order food for everyone from a local tavern.

This meant that the team connected on both a social and a professional level, creating a team spirit, instead of being just disconnected workers who happened to be in the same lab. This practice of a midnight lunch transformed employees into colleagues and it served as the foundation for collaboration in all of Edison's labs.

He realized as a teenager that collaboration was the best way to success. He went on to create what he believed to be the perfect environment to foster both collaboration and innovation. Collaboration is most powerfully generated in small, diverse teams, with both experts and generalists present on the team, and it begins with collegiality. Unless people feel they can roll up their sleeves and work together, innovation can be illusive.

Collaboration evolves from a shared context of learning, not the mere execution of a list of tasks. Through discovery learning, a collaborative team develops content they hold in common. It is reinforced as much through casual chatting, as it is through formal agendas.

Collaboration serves as the invisible glue that allows innovation to advance and sustain momentum. Without collaboration, innovation stalls. Edison mentored his colleagues by always ensuring they felt like part of his team and that they were essential for bringing about the innovative collaboration needed to bring new ideas to life.

Ski Pants and Appreciation

As a mom, whenever we had a big snowfall, I jumped right on the sled with the kids so that we could all share the experience together. While at times it is necessary to let kids experience things on their own, other times, it is often best to dive right in and join them because those are relationship-building moments we will probably treasure forever.

In business, any great leader should have an understanding of how each department functions and should spend time learning its fundamentals and getting to know each team. Know the business intimately. We can't be afraid to get our hands dirty along with the team. We should be comfortable writing sales materials, running the numbers, testing the software, helping to select the merchandise, or even loading the trucks. Those are the opportunities to really understand the business and build relationships with employees that create a strong tie.

It is a basic human need to want to be acknowledged and appreciated. Appreciating others and being grateful is as important in business as it is at home. Never forget to thank anyone who has helped, done work or offered counsel. Businesses are built, and lost, this way. When things are tough, and they often are in the trenches of innovation, appreciating what we have goes a long way toward renewing energy and enthusiasm. As a mentor and inspirer of innovation, don't let the team forget the value of gratitude, each and every day.

Take Away Tips

- Mentors make a difference, inspiring, nurturing, protecting and connecting innovators.
- Mentors should help create a safe environment to fail fast, often and forward.
- The best mentors make us want to exceed expectations – theirs and ours.
- Mentors listen as much as they advise, without judgment.
- We're never too old to be mentored; seek out those who will help spark the magic of innovation.

Inspiring Innovation

Inspiring Innovation

Section Three

Innovation Implemented

Chapter Five

The Power of Associative Logic

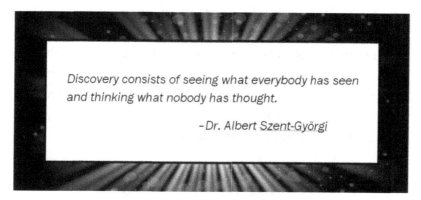

> *Discovery consists of seeing what everybody has seen and thinking what nobody has thought.*
>
> *–Dr. Albert Szent-Györgi*

There are many things that factor into fostering innovation. We have explored various elements from historical facts to the power of mentorship and the importance of allowing people the freedom to fail. However, as we begin to imagine implementing the concept of innovation, there is one key secret that is vital to success: the ability to use associative logic.

What is associative logic? Associative logic means we put things together in surprising and unexpected ways to solve dilemmas, address challenges, and open up new horizons. For business purposes, it is typically defined as a process "involved in discerning and applying connections between unrelated or distantly related concepts" (everything2.com).

Innovation can come from uncovering something completely breakthrough and new to the world, but it can also come from a simpler place – right in front of our very eyes. Dr. Albert Szent-Györgi, a Nobel Prize winning cancer researcher and author, reminds us, in his quote, to look again at what we've already seen, only from a different perspective. Dr. Szent-Gyorgi researched the role of muscle contraction and energy, fostering many important discoveries. I like to think of associative logic as an important muscle in the discovery and understanding of new ideas and opportunities.

Identifying the Power of Associative Logic

In his book *Blink,* Malcolm Gladwell talks of the power of thinking without thinking. His take on the concept of associative logic is that great decision makers are not those people who process the most information or spend the most time deliberating, but those who have perfected the art of thin-slicing – filtering the very few factors that matter from the overwhelming number of variables in any given situation and putting them into action.

To create an environment that inspires innovation and to truly benefit from associative logic, companies and organizations must value and reward it. We have to incentivize re-looking at former thinking, reviewing existing data and hypotheses, and putting the pieces together in new ways. We have to prize collaborating even when collaboration might seem counter-intuitive, when teams might have cross-purposes.

We need to teach each other how to do use associative logic in a methodical way. It is sometimes a bit like slogging through the mud as we comb through research, but it can often be fun and enlightening, too.

While new thinking is important, it's also critical not to neglect former thinking. There are so many instances where an incredible idea has already been thought of, or even tried, but it was ahead of its time. Perhaps it was not communicated clearly, over-ruled by a team with different priorities, or simply lost in the shuffle of changing people, roles or budgets.

Questioning the Past to Build the Future

Often innovation challenges are presented as competitive threats, a fear that we aren't differentiated enough or won't be differentiated as the marketplace evolves. They are a desire to get and stay ahead of the curve. Sometimes they are wide-open fields yet to be addressed, essentially white space opportunities.

Other times, innovation is considered the necessary common course of action and a continuous pipeline of new and different is required. The foundational grounding in what we already know should be the first step in associative logic. No matter how new the frontier, we always know something. So beginning with an assessment of what we know is a great place to start. It helps to demystify and diminish uncertainty as we kick off the thinking process.

I always recommend asking our team and ourselves what do we already know? Here's an initial framework:

- What do we know about our consumer?
- What do we know about our consumer, customer or influencer?
- What do we know about the marketplace, industry, category or related or analogue categories?
- What do we know about the environment – regulatory, geopolitical, scientific or technological influences?
- What do we know about what we bring to the party?

Inspiring Innovation

Think equally about:

- Our brand equity (if it already exists)
- Our positioning (or potential positioning)
- Our strengths and weaknesses; an initial SWOT (strengths, weaknesses, opportunities, threats) analysis is helpful here if we are beginning with an existing business or proposition.
- Our technology and process advantages
- What do we know about our competition, current and anticipated?
- What have we learned recently and what are its implications?
- What partnerships have been successful and why?
- What resources can we access today?
- What big questions can't we answer yet? For these questions, make a list and a learning plan.

When asking these questions, do it with no bias or prejudice. First, just gather information. Read voraciously – whatever is publicly available (there's a lot) or what's been custom-developed. Look for kernels worth exploring and note them along the way. Look for things that show up as a potential opportunity, an area to exploit, a past big win or big loss. Don't hesitate to focus on work done in the past and abandoned. Lay everything out and then begin to match it to other nuggets, especially those that don't seem to fit together. Looking internally at disconnects and trying to connect them is valuable. Looking externally and broadly can be even more fruitful and can spark ideas.

It is important to think across typical boundaries. While there is a role for specialization, at Luminations we think we are better innovators because of the breadth of our experiences. We like to say that working across many industries, channels, models and technologies opens vistas that as a specialist we might not see.

For instance, monitoring changing tastes for spices could lead to a compelling idea for an ingredient in facial skin care. Today, as we think about innovation in digital health, we also evaluate non-health-care-related technologies that might bring parallels. Interactions with our digital devices are changing rapidly and by looking at other countries', we may gain new ideas. The WeChat shake in China might be helpful in North America and the voice interaction found in other countries is making a big impact in the U.S. today.

Case Study

A few years ago, we worked on an initiative to innovate in the artificial hip category. The innovation wasn't about the product per se but the business model and how potential patients came to consider a joint replacement. The client wanted to do more to capture consumers early in their journey toward joint replacement surgery. Patients were said to be on the continuum of "first twinge to ultimate replacement hinge".

Marrying this desire up with an understanding of how another of their portfolio companies captured and engaged consumers early in a journey was extremely beneficial. Their other company spoke to new moms from the moment they found out they were pregnant until they had their baby and beyond. Both groups sought a like-minded community and expert advice. Both faced medical and nonmedical complexities.

While the consumer was very different and the patient journey time frame was different (9 months vs. 9 years), the motivation to gather information and connect with other similar "sufferers" was the same. The reward for providing information that would ultimately lead to brand and purchase decisions was also similar. In the end, the results of wooing these consumers or patients early were equally profitable.

Inspiring Innovation

Associative Logic Lessons

A great example of looking at old things in a new way is the creation of Kraft blue box Macaroni and Cheese. This is such an American staple that we cannot picture a time when it did not exist.

J.J. Kraft began his business back in 1903 with $65 and horse and wagon. It was a simple concept. He purchased cheese and used his horse and wagon to deliver it to local merchants. His brothers joined him in the business. By 1915, they had expanded and began making processed cheese in a tin that was used by the U.S. Government as troop rations during World War I.

Kraft could have just continued to reap the benefits of getting a head start from all the government sales. However, as legend goes, it was a smart-thinking plant employee at Kraft that came up with the idea that has now become such an American family favorite.

The factory that made the processed cheese was always covered in cheese dust. At the end of each day it was simply swept up and thrown away. After seeing a peddler trying to sell bags of cheap pasta with a bag of grated cheese attached, this unexpected innovator proposed the idea of packaging the cheese powder in a foil envelope, and putting it in a box with inexpensive pasta. Kraft Mac and Cheese was born.

The new product was launched in 1937 at the height of the Great Depression. People were cash poor and starving all across America, so this inexpensive but good product was welcome. Their slogan back then was "make a meal for four in nine minutes – all for 19 cents."

This was a product that was created through the innovations brought forward by associative logic. A staff member saw the waste in the factory, put the idea together with what a peddler was selling, and the idea was generated. The owner of Kraft had the presence of mind to recognize a great idea when he saw one and gave the green light to manufacture and promote the new product. Add the creative negotiation with the government to sell two boxes for one ration card, and an American tradition emerged. Almost 100 years after it was created, the business is still around.

Craisins® are another example of successful associative logic. When Ocean Spray was making cranberry juice and sauces, they left behind tons of cranberry hulls. They paid companies to haul the hulls away and discard them. The cooperative knew there was a demand for cranberries in baking but fresh cranberries were only available during a short window each year. At the same time, dried fruit continued to grow in popularity as a snack. Fruit began to top salads and became a sought-after ingredient in new, healthier recipes. They put a task force together to figure out what to do with this by-product.

The team came up with the concept of adding back a little juice to these hulls and selling them as baking ingredients. Later, they entered the snack market too. Obviously, they didn't want to call them squished cranberries or hulls. Dried grapes were called raisins and so they decided to call them Craisins®. Craisins® are now one of the largest selling items in the Ocean Spray line. They say that revolutionizing blueberries is next. As with cheese dust, left over and discarded materials can be turned into big business, all through the use of associative logic.

Leaps of Logic Bring Two Industries Together

After the Exxon Valdez horrific oil leak, companies were scrambling to help clean up the environment. Almost eleven million gallons of oil had spilled into Prince William Sound. One manufacturer had built a thin material that absorbed massive quantities of oil when placed on the surface of the water.

After a year of clean up, the surface oil was gone but the company had overproduced these gigantic oil-absorbing sheets. They started applying associative logic and imagined other categories where the material could be effective – where else could oil be removed? After exploring the auto industry, they arrived at my office at J & J.

At the time, I was overseeing Johnson & Johnson's new acne brand, Clean & Clear®. What if, they asked, we could use this material for facial oil? Sheets to sop up facial oil – it was a far-fetched idea in those days, or was it? In Asia, people used a blotting paper with powder to absorb oil. Putting the technology from the Exxon Valdez to work on potential acne sounded like an effective torture test.

We cut the sheets into small 2-inch by 2-inch squares and tested a concept of facial cleansing sheets. The product was a hit, and Clean & Clear Oil-absorbing sheets were launched. Thinking about oil absorption in a diversity of industries engendered this new idea. For those who experience facial oil, it's a fun and effective way to eliminate it and the product is still on the shelf over twenty years after we first brought it to consumers.

Looking Carefully at Fads and Trends

Another place to search when applying associative logic is with fads and trends. A fad is usually something that flairs up in popularity for six months or a year and then vanishes. A trend is a something much bigger, long-term, and encompasses many layers of consumer attention.

One of the more famous fads when I was young was the Pet Rocks craze. They were the brainchild of advertising executive Gary Dahl back in 1975. Based on hearing other people complain about having to look after pets, he decided to create a Pet Rock, complete with a carry case and a booklet of instructions. It was all the rage for the Christmas season of 1975, but faded away by 1976.

A similar fad in the present day is fidget spinners. Yes, you can get them in different themes, colors and designs, but they are all essentially constructed the same way and are meant for a few minutes of amusement by children. While some kids pride themselves on collecting them, my guess is that by next year, fidget spinners will have gone the way of Pet Rocks. A fad might lead to an idea but a trend can take us to a bigger, more sustainable one.

Matching up learning, data, trends, and behavior from completely diametrically opposed categories and finding the inherent connections that spark ideas; this is the power of associative logic. Highlight connections that can uncover a big idea, discoveries that everyone has seen before but never looked at in quite this way.

For example, do snack foods and jewelry have parallels? Both are often seen as an indulgence – a way to reward oneself. Is there something to be learned from the snack food category that will help a popular jewelry company innovate around helping consumers indulge themselves more? My guess is that there are certainly connections if we look hard enough.

One major trend we are observing right now is tracking of our personal metrics. We now have the capability to track in a very different way than just a few years ago: reliably and digitally. So, we keep track of our numbers. We may want to track quality of sleep, or the number of steps in a day. People might monitor their pulse or respiration rate. North American consumers may look at their data daily, hourly or even more frequently. People can collect it and monitor and leverage data in ways that they never have before. They can create habits, change habits, or reinforce behaviors.

Consumers often take action, with a purchase or behavioral change, based on the facts they have collected. In health and personal care, that's a trend that is very important to consider. As we innovate, we now integrate metrics and tracking whenever it makes sense. We believe this is a trend, not just a fad. An actionable trend has the power to influence behavior, products, services, and channels. A trend is a fad with staying power.

Inspiring Innovation

Associative Logic Can Turn a Fad into a Trend

I remember reading an article about toys and why some things become fads and some things become trends. The featured toy store owner in this story claimed that she'd seen some fads turn into trends because people in the know actively nurtured them along.

For instance, from her perspective, Beanie Babies® became a toy trend and not just a fad, because the company that invented them, Ty®, invested in a sales force that went out and talked to toy store owners to understand what consumers were seeking. This helped Ty® to release a different collection of animals every year. They would actually cut off the quantity of the most desirable beanies and under-manufacture deliberately to create demand around certain characters. This planned scarcity, especially for a collector's item, and the spirit of a scavenger hunt was desirable when seeking that next purchase.

When a character didn't sell, Ty® immediately put feet on the street to understand why. They would then make changes based on their findings, always to ensure that Beanie Babies stayed relevant and continued as a longer-term trend instead of fizzling out in six months like the Pet Rock did. They looked for real insights among buyers and shop owners and this helped sustain the trend.

Back to the concept of fidget spinners--we can go to a digital marketplace and order fidget spinners from China. For the moment, it appears that they are all essentially the same and nobody is really thinking about the insight behind why they became popular. Maybe we should think about the insight behind them. What did a fidget spinner mean and why was it so appealing to students? How come it spread so fast? Was this purely viral social media or was there more to it? Nobody appears to be doing real analysis and managing the fad into a trend like Ty® did with Beanie Babies. Could there be a deeper consumer insight that was missed—students increasing

66

need for stimuli perhaps? Therefore, they will likely end up as a simple fad, not a trend.

A fun fashion fad I have been watching closely, recently, is the popularity of booties in women's footwear. Fashion themes are very often fast-moving fads and not long-term trends. In this case, booties provide a much more comfortable high heel option with dresses and skirts than pumps and sandals. They don't have the exact look of heels but have, fortunately, grown in popularity. I hope that this will become a long-term trend as they are much more comfortable than spike heels for a professional woman's wardrobe. At first glance, because there seems to be a real insight behind them (attractive look but much more comfort), there's a shot that they might become a trend.

Mega Trends

Apple has sparked many of what I would call mega trends. They brought personal computers to the marketplace, back when most computers filled a room, not a book bag. Another trend Apple pioneered is the concept of curating our own music collection, first on popular devices such as the IPod, released in 2001.

Despite Apple's current success, not many people remember that the company's first handheld device was the Newton, released in 1993. People don't remember because the Newton was a flop. If Apple had not been such a forward-thinking company, they would have left the handheld device market and missed out on a multi-billion-dollar industry. They learned from the flop and kept innovating; an earlier example of failing fast but forward.

While Facebook was not the first social media platform, it catapulted the idea into the mainstream. Sharing key moments in life, via social media, is now a mega trend, with billions of people using thousands of platforms worldwide. I don't believe we'll ever return to the days of personal privacy.

Inspiring Innovation

Using Fads and Trends as a Springboard to Innovation

Capitalizing on fads and trends, as a springboard for innovation, means moving very rapidly and having your antenna up all the time. This includes looking at both traditional and non-traditional sources of information.

For us, whenever we're doing an innovation project, we conduct what we call a Luminations Searchlight SocialScan ™. This casts the net very widely in publicly available data online. This search would incorporate chat communities, bulletin boards, forums, websites, and social listening to understand the dialogue around a category or product or need state. It is amazing what we can pick up by listening.

One widely-available way to keep a finger on the pulse of what is happening is Google trends. Last year, Google predicted the increasing incidence of cold and flu, in certain markets, ahead of the Fan flu index, a well-known industry service for companies that make products related to cough, cold, and respiratory care. This Fan flu service had an algorithm that tracked diagnosed cases, and then forecasted future incidence in certain concentric circles around those geographies. Google just looked at the number of cold and flu symptoms searched in a certain geography, and they could predict, based on the number of questions entered into Google, where the incidences of flu were popping in a particular market.

Instead of having to pay for flu data, a respiratory care or a cold and flu product or a vitamin C brand could get that information from Google simply by asking in what markets are we seeing the most questions about symptoms? Sore throat, sneezing, coughing? Google Trends is a free service.

By using digital tools, it is possible to monitor trends constantly. However, it is equally important to be attuned to the physical world. That means not sitting at a desk, but getting out into the physical world to see what is trending.

So, if we're working on skin care, we'll spend time in various retail environments, up-and-coming retail as well as traditional food, drug and mass outlets. We would go to dermatologist offices, salons, spas, but also to other places that might not be considered cutting edge for skin care. We'd explore spots where products might emerge, whether that's craft shows or state fairs, or natural food stores. We might throw a home-based selling party to explore that range of products or find niche products online. So many brands and innovations start by testing and selling online. The barriers to entry and sales are much less burdensome so testing the water is easier than in the past. It's a fertile place to explore.

Looking Across Industries Fosters Innovation

Looking across channels and across industries can foster innovation from some surprising sources. For instance, when it comes to baby skin care or hair care, we often look at innovations in pet care. There are a lot of similarities between the parents of babies and the owners (or parents) of a pet. The actual user of the product cannot say what he or she wants, so the parents decide for them.

The end benefits of the product may make the baby or the pet feel better, but the parent must feel good about what they're doing for that baby or pet, as well. So, turning to analogue categories, products and services makes a lot of sense.

We might look at trending flavors as we think about fragrances. This is vital for the home fragrance industry, if not for the personal fragrance industry. Conversely also, we might look at fragrances if we're thinking about new flavors. What does pumpkin smell like? Well, commercially today, it usually smells like cinnamon and vanilla with hints of nutmeg. But in reality, plain pumpkin does not smell like that at all.

When we buy pumpkin coffee, or pumpkin muffins, or pumpkin anything, what we're buying is a feeling of comfort and warmth and harvest and autumn. So, the question, when companies started formulating pumpkin flavors, was what fragrances and flavors signify those attributes? Cinnamon and vanilla are two such flavors and fragrances and that's why those are commonly wrapped around pumpkin. This is all part of the intricacy of looking at fragrance for flavor, and flavors for fragrance, an association it's valuable to understand.

Applying Associative Logic

Several years ago, I was looking for an au pair for my youngest son and I began searching on a website that matched trusted childcare providers with clients. Au pairs are international students, aged 18-26, who want to come work as childcare providers for 1-2 years. I realized I was only considering au pairs that had uploaded a video. In a video, I got a very different experience than I got from a written profile. I could hear their voices and see when they were interacting with kids. Most of them filmed themselves driving, and I could see in what environment they were driving, and how comfortable they seemed. The video connection made me feel a lot more reassured about selecting an au pair candidate.

At the same time as I was searching for a new au pair, I found myself making a foray into the world of online dating. I hadn't dated in 26 years and my impending divorce threw me back into it. I found most online dating sites gave me no reassurances. Profiles were often fake or embellished. There was no way to check the authenticity of the profile, which was a written statement not a video, and maybe a photo. I couldn't be sure if the photo was truly the person he said he was. These profiles just didn't bring me close to a connection the way a short video would. These conclusions led to the development of an online dating site with video profiles, VerEdates, which is still in beta testing. The associative logic of connecting on video in selecting a babysitter led to an idea for a very different application of video profiles.

It is important to keep looking at analogue categories. Even those that may not be trying to solve the same problem. Beyond a scan of digital and physical environments exploring analogue categories help too.

Listen to the Experts

Faith Popcorn is someone who has made a career out of being a futurist, someone who has the ability to identify sustainable consumer trends and translate the business opportunity for the benefit of her clients at her firm Brain Reserve.

One of my chief designers for many years came from Brain Reserve, so obviously I'm a believer. But what she accomplished and what other experts are doing is effectively synthesizing what they see happening in the world. It is beneficial to know, understand, and leverage what experts and thought leaders have to say.

A couple years back we were working for a brand of very wonderful, natural skin care products called Korres. Most of their new ingredients came from new applications of plant extracts. In this instance it was important to bring in botanists and scientists who truly understood plant extracts and what they could do for human skin. The expert wasn't just a dermatologist or a cosmetologist, but somebody who was thinking about rare plants and plant extracts, and trying to discover what hadn't been discovered yet. Without these experts, new ingredients and their benefits would not have been revealed. Innovation often means looking at what we already know differently. It also means admitting what we don't know and asking thoughtful questions, leaning on experts, and shamelessly pursuing knowledge to build upon.

Creative Application of Associative Logic

When it comes to the application of associative logic in the world of innovation, we need team members who can truly look at a situation from all possible perspectives. This is especially critical when it comes to turning a failed project into a success. A prime example of this is the Post-It® note. Popular culture has the story as an a-ha moment. In actual fact, the progression of this office necessity took over a decade. The original mistake happened in 1968 when Dr. Spencer Silver, a scientist at 3M, accidentally created a low-tack adhesive when he was really trying to develop a super-strong adhesive.

Over the years, Dr. Silver promoted his new product within 3M, even bringing it up in seminars. In 1974, Art Fry attended one of these seminars, and he tried using the low-tack adhesive to keep his bookmark from falling out of his hymn book. Fry then used 3M's officially-sanctioned bootlegging policy to develop the idea further. The original yellow color was also a happenstance, as the lab next door to his office only had yellow scrap paper for him to borrow.

The launch of press and peel notes in 1977 was disappointing, but when 3M decided to issue free samples to a large market in 1979, 94 percent of the participants said they would buy the product. The re-launch, under the Post-It® brand, happened in 1980 and it went on to become a worldwide phenomenon worth over $1 billion.

Another example of cross-industry application of associative logic is the discovery of the hair regrowth benefits of Rogaine®. This active ingredient was initially designed in pill form as a treatment for high blood pressure. When they began clinical testing, patients noticed that a side effect was increased hair growth. Because the medicine was ingested, hair regrowth happened all over the body, often in unwanted spots. They imagined targeted hair regrowth and put the minoxidil into a lotion to be applied to the head. While they did continue to develop the compound in pill form for high blood pressure, they also launched the topical application for re-growing hair in male pattern baldness and ultimately for women as well. Today Rogaine®, or Regaine® outside the U.S., is part of a $4B category.

Priming the Pump

Many companies today invest in sending team members to CES, the fabled computer electronics show in Las Vegas. People attend even if they have nothing to do with technology or industries that they perceive to be benefiting from the technology showcased at CES. Why? It opens minds to different possibilities and to unlock creativity differently. I recommend attending at least once every few years.

Other types of conferences and venues inspire different ideas. Allow teams to get out and experience conferences and shows and showcases, as well as training and development, potentially even in unrelated areas. This will expand horizons. Always support the team in their quest for data and for fulfilling their curiosity. Many of the people interviewed for this book listed curiosity as a key characteristic in successful innovators. Mentors should connect them with others in an organization that might be able to provide knowledge, or invest in contracts that will allow them to get information.

There are certain parts of the world, too, where I always look for the next big thing. For instance, when we think about mindfulness and meditation and balance, India comes to mind. If I'm looking for innovation in health care technology, I might look to Israel. They put a lot of brainpower and investment into the sector, and often Israeli investors and entrepreneurs think broadly without letting themselves get bogged down in all details that may hinder them. They are trained young to be decisive yet take risks. Whereas we're much more comfortable in our routines here in the US, and sometimes it is harder for us to think beyond the traditional. The magic comes from allowing us to be inspired by experts, trends, new categories and surprises. We need to open our minds by opening our doors and getting outside.

Take Away Tips

- Associative logic is putting seemingly disparate and disconnected ideas together in new and fruitful ways.
- Trends have staying power and are based in real consumer insight while fads are temporary.
- Applying associative logic helps uncover surprising opportunities.
- Get out of the office and outside a comfort zone to get beyond incremental ideas.

Inspiring Innovation

Chapter Six

Brainstorming for Innovation

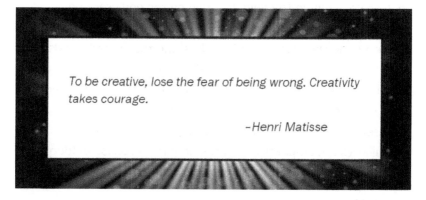

> To be creative, lose the fear of being wrong. Creativity takes courage.
>
> —Henri Matisse

According to Dictionary.com, the definition of brainstorming is "a conference technique of solving specific problems, amassing information, stimulating creative thinking, and developing new ideas, by unrestrained and spontaneous participation in discussion." Traditionally, brainstorming was a way to create a safe environment so that all team members felt they could express themselves and no idea was too outrageous.

While brainstorming is a vital ingredient of true innovation, brainstorming without any structure can be a recipe for disaster.

The truly effective brainstorm finds that happy middle ground where many ideas flow toward a common goal.

Brainstorming the Google Way

Google has been on the cutting edge of business innovation since they began in 1998. While they made the news with their innovative search engine and their new approach to company culture, along the way they also came up with their own approach to brainstorming.

From their perspective, Google thought that brainstorming could be better. Their process was very specific, it was a linear course meant to take new ideas and turn them into actual products and it had three parts:

Step 1: Know the User

So, Google begins in the field, focusing on the end user and collecting stories, emotions and ideas. They take the view that as a company, they need to not only understand their users' needs, they need to be able to relate to them. Members of their team would travel the world over and get input from many users in different countries and they always make sure that, the end user is represented in any official brainstorming session. This is not dissimilar to the empathize or gather inspiration phase of Ideo®'s Design Thinking method.

Step 2: 10x

Once they feel that they know the user destination, its time to think 10x. This concept is focused on improving something by 10x not just 10%. It's about bringing magnitude to the table. They keep pushing to make sure the idea is big enough.

Once the brainstorming has begun the process kicks into high gear with the application of the following six guidelines:

1. It's easy to kill an idea, so follow up with "yes and" instead of "no but" and build on each other's ideas.
2. Generate lots of ideas. Quality is more important than quantity, so really let loose. The best way to have a great idea is to have many ideas.
3. Write short headlines. Being able to describe an idea in less than six words helps clarify it. Imagine a favorite media outlet or magazine covers this great idea: What would the headline say?
4. Illustrate. Pictures are usually louder than words and harder to misinterpret.
5. Think big. Invite bold, intrepid ideas—yes, this is the "10x" part—not little, incremental solutions. As Frederik Pferdt, Google's head of innovation and creativity, said, "Just beyond crazy is fabulous."
6. Defer judgment. Don't judge ideas in the midst of brainstorming (remember Rule #1) but let them grow and iterate.

Step 3: Prototype – Make it happen

The final step, of course, is to take action and create something. The problem with many brainstorming sessions is that they end with an agreement to have yet another meeting later-that can be a mistake. It's essential to strike when the iron is hot and take action quickly. Google invests in fast prototyping to get a product or software into users' hands rapidly.

Back at the Beginning

I started Luminations as a company before I left my job as CEO at Netgrocer back in the early 2000's. It was started because I was observing a trend, a problem that I thought I could help solve, in my community. That trend was that many small businesses in Hillsborough, New Jersey, were failing.

Inspiring Innovation

The businesses themselves had a lot to offer, but the business owners, who had various skills such as chef, or party planner or Tae Kwon Do instructor, lacked the marketing skills to actually generate enough business to survive. A number of decent businesses run by talented people were closing in town and there were a lot of retail stores where we could see through from front to back as they were now, sadly, unoccupied.

As a member of the community, I patronized a lot of these businesses and I was sad to see them go. I started asking, "Why are you going out of business?". The answers I got were 1) not enough traffic, 2) not enough sales, 3) services weren't profitable – the bottom line was just not enough business to stay viable.

It occurred to me that what most of the businesses needed was creative marketing thinking and planning. I started Luminations to help local businesses who needed some big company marketing thinking but couldn't afford it.

Since I was doing a lot of the work pro bono, I occasionally bartered my services, but I created an umbrella company just to house the cost of developing websites and brand names and marketing plans for companies. That was happening behind the scenes and the reward was just having the pottery-painting place in town for my kids to visit, or the Tae Kwon Do studio that the whole family could continue to attend.

When Netgrocer was sold, my 3rd child was six months old and I thought that I would take a maternity leave because I hadn't really taken one when he was born. Before departing, I asked the management team to join me in the warehouse to help organize the remaining inventory before we left the company. This was the day before Thanksgiving in 2002. In the warehouse, I tripped and broke my elbow.

So, between having a relatively new baby and a broken elbow, I thought it was a sign that I should take some time off. My plan was to take a break and then start applying for jobs. But instead, the day after Thanksgiving, a former colleague called me and said, "I need new concepts, global new concepts in oral care, and I need 20 of them fast. I remembered that that was a strength of yours and is there any way you could do this for me?"

I thought hard about how I could do it. I had a broken elbow so I wasn't even sure if I could type and I had been relishing the idea of taking some time off. Still, I was very excited by the opportunity to generate innovations in oral care. And, of course, it was flattering that somebody had called me and remembered me for that skill set so, I offered to take a stab.

When it came time to invoice the client for my concepts, I decided to do it under the umbrella of Luminations and that became the first paid project for Luminations. The good news is that the concepts tested extremely well. They were some of the highest testing concepts J&J had ever seen in oral care.

That team recommended me to another team that happened to be women's health, an area near and dear to my heart as well. This was a similar project that involved really digging deeply into the consumer research to uncover addressable insight, and brainstorming ideas that would build the business.

That was my second official Luminations project and after that I never looked back. I never did go on any job interviews. I started doing more innovation and new product development work right after that and soon brought some other really talented folks to my team.

Our approach to developing breakthrough ideas was, at first, somewhat haphazard, using the fundamentals of what I knew to do, but not implementing it in any formal way, not creating a real process. During those first couple of years, we developed a much more formal framework and roadmap to generating the biggest ideas we could for our clients. That, today, is one of our core offerings and it is called the Luminations Lightning Strike®. Our Lightning Strike® is the foundation for much of the innovation work that we do. We offer a virtual Luminations Lightning Strike® process and a physical, in-person, Lightning Strike® brainstorm process.

Over the past fifteen years, Luminations has become a catalyst for brainstorming across a wide range of industries and organizations. Our process is designed to develop big ideas that are actionable.

At Luminations, we don't just give a client a binder of ideas they can put on the shelf, we give them ideas that are immediately executable. Innovation just for the sake of innovation does not help build businesses, and that's not what we do. Every creative act starts with a purpose.

The Luminations Lightning Strike® Process

After completing several major innovation projects involving massive amounts of background information and the generation of award-winning results, we began to analyze how this magic was happening. There are three key components to a strong Lightning Strike® which we call the three D's or 3D's:

1. The Discovery process where a breadth of information was reviewed, absorbed, sorted and catalogued.
2. The Distillation of all this information into key observations and implications and importantly, a creative brainstorm brief, for the future deliverables.
3. The Delivery – the fine-tuning the results to arrive at the end goal; the actual creative ideation leading to themes and new concepts for our clients.

Phase 1: Discovery: The discovery process is a deep dive into all of the existing information the client may have and any incremental information we can find through our Searchlight Social Scan® process, looking online, looking at historical data, looking at competitive information, and casting a wide net. Here is where we spend time with that long list of questions from Chapter 5 and our SocialScan® review.

There is so much information publicly available today, that this step can be challenging to manage. Our first job is to find and gather all of the relevant data in one place. This includes interviewing any of the key stakeholders and/or client team members. Once all this information is assembled, it's time to move on to Phase 2.

Phase 2: Distillation: At this point, we begin synthesizing and curating all of that learning. It is an integral part of the brainstorming process. We focus on observations and implications. We have our observations on we've absorbed and then what we think through the implications for the project or challenge.

We then develop a Lightning Strike® brainstorm brief. The brief is a clear restatement of the scope of work that says: this is what we want to accomplish as a team. Everything we do is collaborative and all team members need to align on the brief before moving on.

Because our Lightning Strike® process is always in collaboration with our client, we can rarely point to an innovation and say "that's ours." We might have uncovered the insight. We might have come up with the first kernel of the idea. We may have written the winning concept or even worked on the lead prototype but when we see an innovation on the market, it is always a collaborative effort.

The Lightning Strike® brief is developed to guide the ideation. That brief lays out the target audience for this solution, innovation, message or concept. The target audience can be incredibly narrow or broader, but never so broad as to make it hard to find a meaningful insight and allow for differentiated positioning among them. There might be a primary and secondary target audience. Next in the brief, what is the business objective? If it's a brand, what is the brand objective? What are the key benefits of this idea for the target? What is our client's definition of success and what, if any, are the specific mandatories? Does the learning need to be testable in a certain methodology? Does it have to be compelling enough to get $20 million in funding? Does the work need to encompass multiple countries or regions? If it exists, what is the equity of the global brand and how can we ensure we are consistent?

Next comes our mandatory takeaways and what will our results phase or our deliverable look like? Is it 20 concepts in oral care? Is it a new business model or process in diabetes? Is it a different way of conducting orthopedic surgery that minimizes hemorrhage? Is it leveraging a technology from Japan that must be sold in the U.S.?

What is the key deliverable, and then what does it look like in terms of how we deliver it to the client? It could be a training curriculum for new marketers. It could be a presentation for senior management or it could be concepts for consumers or surgeons or patients. Finally, we list any key supporting claims, studies or technologies. These are the components of our Lightning Strike® brief. Once the brief is agreed upon, based on whether we're doing a virtual Lightning Strike or a physical Lightning Strike, we then conduct the actual brainstorm.

Phase 3: Delivery: Our deliverables are typically not just the ideas themselves but how to help the team get there. The brainstorm could involve putting everybody together in a room, or putting everybody together with a virtual white board. If we are facilitating a physical, in-person session, it is choreographed to the minute from the setup to the stimuli to the desired output to the team assignments.

The participants do not always know the details of any behind-the-scenes choreography, but they do feel that there's a lot of organized energy, a bias toward action, and many tools and templates put in place to help them get there. Often our Lightning Strike® brainstorms start with an expert talking about what we need to know or what we've already done so we can build off of that. This gives the session context and a logical starting point.

By the end of a session, physical or virtual, the outputs should start to look like what we said they would. All participants should see immediate value for their time invested. Coming out of the session we curate the results. If needed, we may conduct a booster session among a core team of our innovation experts.,

Often in a brainstorm session, whether it's physical or virtual, lots of ideas come up that are outside the scope of the specific brief. These might be great thoughts for something else the brand or the business is tackling and so we capture all of that and summarize it as well.

We deliver the results and often we are then done with our piece of the puzzle so we don't necessarlly know what the ultimate outcome was for the client. Equally often, we're asked to begin to execute on the ideas that we have delivered. For example, if the ideation session, the brainstorm, was around a promotional plan for raising sponsorships for a Philadelphia-based bike sharing program, they then might say, "Can you help us approach the top ten companies you thought we should approach?"

So, we might join the client team and execute with them. We might change our role from innovator to executor or partner.

Case Study

In the device space around inhalation and asthma, we had a client ask us to help them identify what the future of inhalation of active ingredients might look like in the future. We evaluated, globally, all of the technologies we thought might have application. We brought the client, after the ideation was over, to many of those potential companies and ultimately helped pursue the commercialization of one – a win for both the startup and the larger company. If the Lightning Strike® involves something closer-in and tactical to the client, we're just as able to make a difference as we are with the long term blue sky or white space innovations. One client recently said, "we need to do a better job in a new channel of distribution, specifically U.S. club stores, can you help?" We applied the Lightning Strike® Process to Costco® programs and brought many potential solutions. At that point, the client, who appreciated the ideas asked, "could we make them happen next year in that channel?" And we did.

Lightning Can Strike Anywhere

In the past 15, years my team and I have performed hundreds of Lightning Strike® brainstorming sessions. Each one different, challenging and inspirational to us in new ways. We've done all kinds of work for leading, iconic brands to startup companies. We have been involved in positioning new herbal ingredients in the obesity space to figuring out what to name and how to educate people on setup of flat panel TV's. We've branded treatments for chronic healthcare conditions, online ordering software, and new products in categories from jewelry to chocolate to nutritional beverages to vitamins to high- end spirits and champagne to color cosmetics and fragrance.

One of my favorite Lightning Strikes® involved McCormick Spices and this led to a major innovation for the company. My team was proud to have worked with their team to create something totally new to the home meal prep and spice market.

Case Study

McCormick first became a client in 2006. Known for their passion for flavor, from their humble beginning in one room in 1889 to the present day when they are the country's largest producer of spices, proprietary seasoning blends, herbs, extracts, sauces and marinades, they reinvent flavor decade after decade. Their research and development is driven by the singular goal of taking meals from ordinary to exciting; from good to great.

However, there had been a slowdown in the retail end of their spice business and they were looking for new ideas. One of the obvious concepts that came out of the research was the need for convenience. Parents wanted to provide home cooked meals with new flavors, but time was tight and families were busier than ever. Qualitative and quantitative research indicated that families were bored with the same old meals but trying new ones felt too risky, particularly with kids at home. It was the early stages of recipe databases and McCormick was focused on this as well. Still, the home chef was often reluctant to try new recipes that could require an investment in a whole series of new spice bottles that may never be used again.

Together with the team, we developed the concept of mini/single use spices – just enough for a new recipe. Recipes were straightforward but gave families a chance to experiment with new flavors at a very modest cost. Ultimately, we provided the recipe cards with blister packs of just the spices needed for a family meal. We tested lots of configurations and the winners are now on the market as McCormick® Recipe Inspirations.

Recipe Inspirations make trying McCormick's best recipes and new spices fun and easy. Each packet includes pre-measured McCormick spices and herbs and a collectible recipe card. The consumer only has to add the fresh ingredients and follow the instructions. This made it easy to make a memorable meal for family or friends, without the guilt of takeout or the fear of rejection. Most importantly, this became a huge win for McCormick as sales escalated on the new product.

How Brainstorming Can Pivot a Whole Company

Netgrocer was founded in 1987 by an Israeli entrepreneur, Uri Evan. He planned to create the first online nationwide supermarket. He achieved this, but his vision was way ahead of the times. Not only was the internet infrastructure not yet in place, but the home delivery structure was not yet fully operational either.

Inspiring Innovation

I began as head of marketing at Netgrocer, and then stepped up to CEO only to watch as outside forces caused the near implosion of the company. The owner was smart enough to know his vision was not working fast enough and, through brainstorming, we were able to create the concept of the Endless Aisle®. The insight was uncovered because we found shoppers and retailers alike were coming to Netgrocer to find their hard-to-find favorite items. Soon manufactures were offering their full lines of products to us and directing consumers our way. The only place in the country that stocked every Jell-O® or Crystal Lite® flavor and every form and sku of Similac® baby formula was Netgrocer. Word was starting to spread.

The Endless Aisle® in a nutshell, was software that allowed the local retailer to show its own customers 30,000 more products than what they carried in the physical store. Shoppers could feel they ordered these items from their own local grocery store instead of going to a competitor and retailers and manufacturers could fulfill loyal customers' wishes.

We decided to pitch this idea to Stop and Shop (an Ahold Chain) and after many heartfelt pitches and trips to Quincy, Massachusetts, they said "well, we will give it a try, but only if you put physical ordering kiosks in our store."

We desperately needed a major retailer to sign on for our Endless Aisle® software solution. We needed it because, without it, we would not have been able to gain further investment in the company and sustain the business for the future.

Since this was still 2001 and the U.S. didn't have well-developed broadband service around the country yet and touch pads and kiosks were relatively new to the world, this was no small challenge. If a customer could not find what he or she was looking for, they would leave and go to the competition. What Stop & Shop wanted was to avoid losing this customer. They wanted to keep her in the store, have her place the immediate order and have it shipped directly to her home.

The condition for the test was that we would have to place kiosks in Stop & Shop and we would have to integrate our system and theirs. These kiosks printed a receipt for customers to take to the cash register for their special order. We had to accomplish it in about 3 months from when they agreed they'd test the system for us. We had no choice, so we had to make it happen.

I brought it to the Netgrocer team with confidence even though I had never done anything like it before and our IT people hadn't either. We had just developed the ordering software and we had no idea if we could make an interface that was simple enough to use on a touch screen or a kiosk keyboard. Plus, most of these stores didn't have wireless or even wired internet service yet so we'd have to install that for them, too. Brainstorming how, not if, we'd make it happen helped. We also offered clear and confident communication, a detailed roadmap, and a heavy dose of optimism.

We sourced the kiosks, coded the software, installed cabling and internet in some of the stores and it worked beautifully. It worked partly because we just believed we could do it. That team worked day and night to develop it. Then we all went into the stores and worked 24/7 staffing those new kiosks to make sure that if anything went wrong, it was fixed fast. Early prototyping and ongoing optimization helped.

Fortunately, not too much went wrong. This was because our technology team was stellar. When Stop & Shop publicly announced its partnership expansion with Netgrocer's Endless Aisle®, as is often the case, everyone in the grocery retail world clamored for it. And that's what we needed to thrive.

While this major win kept Netgrocer afloat, two years later we were looking at a challenging future once again. This time, Amazon was our partner and we needed a cash infusion to purchase and inventory enough products to serve their vast number of customers. We were set to be their nationwide grocery provider. Netgrocer shareholders had something else in mind; an exit not a re-investment.

Our brainstorm was around how to keep our new partner, Amazon and their retail customers happy at the same time we fulfilled the wishes of our shareholders. The solution was to split the company in half. A software service provider would buy the Endless Aisle® platform and support brick and mortar grocery and Amazon. A retailer would buy Netgrocer and manage the nationwide online shopping business. The transaction took place in late 2002, teaching me, once again, the power of solid technology, fresh ideas and collaborative brainstorming.

Take Away Tips
- Brainstorming is a way to generate unrestrained ideas in a safe and collaborative way.
- Design Thinking-based brainstorms involve 4 steps: gather inspiration, generate ideas, make them tangible and share the story.
- Google's brainstorms involve 3 steps: know the user, 10x, and prototyping.
- Luminations Lightning Strike® 3-step brainstorms involve the 3D's: discovery, distillation with the brainstorm brief and idea delivery.

Inspiring Innovation

Inspiring Innovation

Chapter Seven

The Pros and Cons of Technology in Innovation

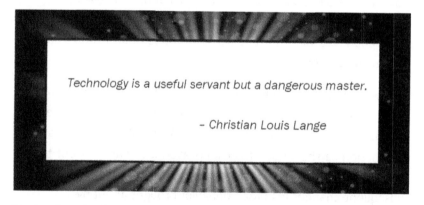

Technology is a useful servant but a dangerous master.

- Christian Louis Lange

Technology in the twenty-first century has moved us quantum leaps forward in terms of being able to access information, get products to market fast and provide an easy means of communication. Along the way, technology has transformed the concept of innovation at its very core.

Technology allows companies to test products and information at speeds and prices that were unimaginable only a few years ago.

We can stick features on websites and tell within hours how customers will respond. We can reach thousands of prospective consumers overnight. We can also 3D print something that might've taken years to prototype if a mold was needed. We can sell without a physical store.

While technology has, for the most part, provided a positive landscape for the development of innovation, there is a downside too. Companies need to be aware of the downside and know how to navigate the paradox that it creates. Technology can also limit us and distract us from seeing real insights and opportunities.

Communication – Pro's and Con's

Technology, in the communication sector, has blossomed almost beyond belief. Cell phones have connected the far-flung corners of our globe. The Internet, bringing the sum-total of human knowledge to everyone's fingertips, provides so many different ways to access this limitless pool of information. In developed nations, the number of personal devices keeps escalating, with smart phones, tablets, notebooks, laptops, computers and smart TVs, to name a few.

Mitchell Kapor, the inventor of Lotus 1-2-3, made an interesting observation when he said, "Getting information off the Internet is like taking a drink from a fire hydrant." While all of this access to information can be a boon to an innovator, it can also disrupt the natural order of things in terms of human communication. The subsequent changes in human behavior brought about by innovations in communication have broad reaching effects both in the social world and the business world.

Changes to Consumer Behavior

Yes, we can now easily access trends, consumer behavior and buying patterns. Being able to harvest information about consumers, getting access to very specific data, gives today's innovators a unique edge. We are able to research our audience and determine exactly what they are looking for in terms of goods and services.

How has behavior changed? Here's a simple example. In the days before the Internet, if we wanted to know if a certain shop was open, we either had to call them or stop by and ask the question in person. Now, we simply google the company, look at their business listing, and know the times they are open. That seems convenient, but think about it. There is now decreased foot traffic in the vicinity of the business. If we had gone down to that shop, chances are we would have seen something there or in another shop window, and we might have already made a purchase.

The changes to buying habits brought about by the internet go far beyond cutting down on foot traffic to brick and mortar stores. Everyone now has access to a global omni channel market and the ability to search and compare. Delivery times have almost caught up with our need for instant gratification. Yet, what are we missing? What display, new product or unique combination of items has passed us by because we are glued to our computer screen or smart phone? What customized selection curated by someone suggesting it, have we skipped. Can Amazon's suggestion engine replace the human factor, that spark that catches our eye? Do we really browse or stumble upon things that might surprise or delight us?

Social Implications

While technology has provided us with a plethora of convenience, there is also an impact on basic social interaction, the flow-on effect to business interactions and the cost to future generations. These are just a few of the areas impacted by advances in communication.

A restaurant in New York City, that had a great reputation, suddenly began to experience a decline in business and increase in complaints about quality and speediness of their service. Puzzled by this feedback, as they had made no major changes in recent times, the restaurant hired a consultant to videotape their service and compare it to videos taken years prior.

The number of customers served on a daily basis was basically the same, but the service seemed slower even though they had cut back on the number of menu items and had added more staff. When they analyzed the two videos, some surprising things came to light.

Back in the days before the arrival of smart phones, a customer would arrive, receive water, get their order, eat and leave within 1 hour and 5 minutes. Now, this same process was taking 1 hour and 55 minutes. Why?

- In 2004, 3 out of 45 customers requested to be seated in a different place. In 2014, 18 out of 45 diners requested to be re-seated.
- In 2004, no one took pictures of their food. In 2014, more than half of the diners took the time to take pictures of their food – sharing takes time.
- In 2004, 2 out of 45 customers sent items back. Ten years later, 9 out of 45 customers sent their food back for reheating (due to all the time taking digital photography, according to the manager).
- In 2004, customers spent an average of eight minutes looking at the menu before closing it to signal they were ready to order. In 2014 it took much longer, as people stopped to text often and then order.
- In 2004, no one asked the waiter to take a group photo. In 2014, 27 out of 45 customers did (and 14 of those requested the waiter to retake the photo).

The bottom line analysis was that the restaurant had not declined in its service – the diners had changed how they interacted with the staff, due primarily to their attention to their phones, social sharing, and a new willingness to make greater demands.

Inspiring Innovation

Basic social interactions, at all levels, have been impacted by the continuous use of smart phones. Instead of greeting each other, many young people may pass each other on the street or in various business settings without even acknowledging each other's existence. Eyes are often glued to their screens. They may miss a smile or the chance to start a conversation. The casual collisions that can lead to fruitful conversation are harder to make happen.

Once upon a time, while sitting in a bar waiting for someone, we would likely strike up a conversation with another patron or even the bartender. Now, chances are, we will stay glued to our device, checking on the various streams of data pouring into our many accounts. We get a lot of data and interact more with people electronically, but it is a profound loss that our face-to-face interactions are declining. As technology overtakes the natural order of things in the social realm, this was inevitable.

Business Interactions

Technology has helped business interactions expand on a global scale. Now, we use Google Hangouts or Skype to hold a team meeting and each participant could be on a different continent. Without the need for frequent travel, we can actually connect better and more often this way.

Digital technology helps innovation just by providing access to people and information that would not otherwise be readily available. Access to information on trends, information on competitors, information on scientific studies, when accessed in a systematic way, can inform and inspire.

Technology also brings about a positive impact in job engagement by providing access to more job resources and distance learning. Recent studies show that individuals are more committed to companies that consistently keep up with new technology. However, it is important not to let technology become a crutch.

Leverage it, but don't use it as an excuse to skip face-to-face interactions.

In The One Thing by Gary Keller, he talks about taking time to discover our one next area of focus and passion. According to him, in order to do that, we cannot be disturbed by technology every five minutes. When technology can interrupt a cadence that might've generated strong ideas, he says to turn it off or put it away. This surely helps the sparks of innovation ignite.

Cloud Technology

In the past several years, cloud computing has become commonplace. We enjoy the benefits and take for granted that we can have cloud storage that can handle immense files in a supposedly secure place. However, recent events have shown that imagining that the cloud is impenetrable is a fallacy. Major hacks have occurred recently, at Experian Credit, Chase, Target and Home Depot.

The downside of overreliance on technology is showcased in aspects of cyber security. Think of all the proprietary data in the cloud that gets hacked and how this could affect innovation. We might come up with the most creative and best idea, but if our cloud storage or online platform is hacked and someone can borrow innovative ideas, then our competitive edge could be jeopardized.

It takes significant effort and investment to stay ahead of the technology curve when it comes to protecting information. With every advancement comes a risk. There are so many damaging types of malware, viruses and new ways to attack other computers. We have to be evolving our skillset constantly and monitoring software to stay ahead of the game. The good news, this creates great upside in the field of cybersecurity, an area we at Luminations enjoy working in.

Impact on the Next Generation

The current generation has grown up taking technology for granted. GPS in cars and on phones are just part of the normal state for anyone under the age of 25. I remember when we had to read a map and keep our wits about us to navigate from one place to another. Having GPS makes life so much easier; however, we have to be careful not to become so dependent on the technology, that we may not know how to navigate without it.

Earlier generations got lost often and developed the skills of knowing how to read a map, memorized how to get from one place to another, and when all else failed, stopped and asked for directions at a gas station. I asked a teenager if he knew the directions to a friend's local high school and he wasn't sure but questioned why he'd need to have this memorized in the first place. He could be right.

Still, solving the problem of how to get somewhere by knowing more than one approach or route is a form of innovation. If we were totally dependent on technology, we wouldn't develop those other navigational skills. Getting lost without access to technology is actually an opportunity to explore. However, a GPS makes us more comfortable in uncharted territory. Both are important.

How Technology Expands Possibilities

When it comes to the consumer world, technology has had a profound effect. With the advent of the internet, it is now possible to research, learn and compare any product or service. Online sites like Trivago and Expedia have revolutionized the hospitality industry by enabling consumers to select hotels and travel plans after uncovering and comparing all possible options.

Technology has also made the selection and purchase of all consumer goods available at the click of a button with split-second access to entire industries. Advances in delivery options have brought the wonder of same day delivery from online giants like Amazon.

3D printers are now printing complex objects, and in a test case, they are even able to print an entire house. Things we thought to be in the realm of science fiction are now becoming a reality.

I recently answered a survey where I was asked if I would let an employer insert a microchip into my hand. I said that I might, because I could see the convenience of not having to look for an id card to swipe to get through a door. I could use it to pay for lunch, or get into the gym. It would be the size of a grain of rice, injected into my hand.

On the other hand, the chip means the company would also know where I was at all times. It might eventually have my health information, medical footprint, and more. As a young woman, maybe I wouldn't want the company to know if I were pregnant quite so early in the game. Yet, imagine the convenience a chip could afford us. If a person were unconscious, a quick scan could provide her medical history. A lost child could be tracked and found.

While technology will continue to expand possibilities, it also continues to raise questions concerning ethics, privacy, freedom, and social behavior. We must balance the concept of efficiency and convenience with the concept of Big Brother – how much is too far?

The Human Element

There are things that machines will never do. They'll never strike out of a little league game and they'll never fall in love and have their heart broken. No matter how automated technology gets, it can only amass and sort data. Even with machine learning and artificial intelligence, I believe that it takes a human brain to make the leaps from patterns and the insights in the data to new ideas and innovation. Some would dispute this. Yes, technology provides the tools and the access to information, but it is still the innovative human that connects all the dots.

For me, the trick is to learn how to use technology for its advantages and benefits. At the same time we should proceed with caution and consider the risks. If we rely on technology it both helps us connect yet at the same time helps hinder our ability to connect in person.

When it comes to innovation, technology needs to remain a well-controlled tool that we use to get to where we need to go. Technology cannot overshadow the inner human magic necessary to create the spark of innovation.

Take Away Tips

- Expand technology horizons as far as possible with new data and tools.
- Beware of information overload – technology can turn on the fire hydrant of information.
- Don't let new technologies erode real live social interactions—essential to innovation.

Chapter Eight

Magical Thoughts on Innovation from Industry Leaders

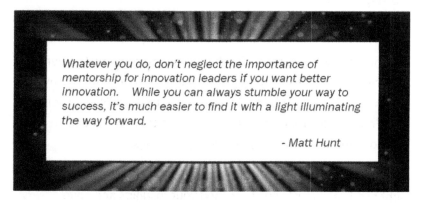

Whatever you do, don't neglect the importance of mentorship for innovation leaders if you want better innovation. While you can always stumble your way to success, it's much easier to find it with a light illuminating the way forward.

- Matt Hunt

I have been extraordinarily lucky over the course of my career to have worked with some incredibly talented leaders and innovators. I was able to interview several thought leaders who reinforced many of the themes in this book.

While some innovators were able to speak publicly, others felt the need to remain anonymous. In all cases, they shared graciously. Many of their ideas inspired my chapters with stories about their mentors, how they created cultures of continuous innovation, protected their teams from derailment and enabled them to fail fast. Most also talked about the importance of structure and process around the creation of ideas. Finally, almost everyone talked about diversity of thought and skills and enduring trust as being integral to the success of their businesses and their teams. Below is just a snapshot of some of the interviews and more will be available online.

Mary Teryek

Vice President at Bausch and Lomb and former Senior Leader in skincare at Valeant and Sandoz

I have known Mary as a client and as a business partner who truly believes in giving her teams autonomy to do what they do best. I was privileged to help her build a skin care line that she eventually sold to L'oreal. My team at Luminations worked with her on that journey.

How Do You Inspire Innovation?

One of the most important things you have to remember when looking at how to inspire innovation is that trust and autonomy are paramount. Leaders need to keep in mind that people on their team often know more than they do – give them the space, freedom and trust and they can do great things.

You have to surround yourself with the right kind of people with the right mind set. Trust your team and your instincts and have confidence in your direction even if others aren't following. Zig when others are zagging.

As a leader in innovation, shepherd the thinking of people who have a vision. I find that progress comes from talking through observations first, then creating a strategy next, then looking hard at the competition – then going in a totally different direction.

How do you find the people who will push innovation?

Mary brings a design and artistic background – art – to the science of marketing which she was able to help apply to the creative process. Recognize and reward the differences in thinking. Give as much freedom as you can to let them move forward – and most of all, allow failure.

Agree to disagree with smart team members and ask them to "prove me wrong, I want to be wrong". Be humble and know others may know more – crowdsourcing generates more ideas than sitting in an ivory tower.

Who Inspires You?

My inspiration came from a high school teacher who believed in my ability to be an artist and helped me get into Carnegie Mellon. No one in the professional world really set me up to succeed until Joe Gordon at Valeant recognized that I had big ideas. He had trust and faith in both my creative and strategic thinking. Don't let the process kill every idea. Joe also trusted that his team might know more than he did, even though that can be hard for a leader to realize.

What advice would you give someone who wants to inspire innovation?

Don't be afraid to let people be who they are and implement just as much process as you need to keep on track, but not more. Set clearly assign roles and responsibilities – accountability with a fluid process is really important. All team members need to feel valued and that they are bringing value. All need to feel invested in the success of the business. At Valeant, we never got punished for a bad idea – we did have some good laughs and a sense of humor is important. Nobody shut down ideas too early they let us try it.

Examples of breakthrough innovation:

We evolved a skin care brand, CeraVe, from 5 sku's to 70 in 4 years – almost every single item is still on the market. The high multiple, when it was acquired by L'oreal, proved the value of innovation. Never forget that innovation drives growth and value.

Ilene Quilty

Innovation Consultant at The Luminations Group

Ilene helped drive incredible innovation at a number of Johnson & Johnson companies. When I first met her, she was developing a kids' hair care line and facing lots of obstacles. She never let any get in her way. From hair care to skin care to wound care, pain and allergy, she contributed to the growth of many businesses during her time at J&J and now I'm fortunate enough to have her on my team.

How Do You Nurture Innovation?

Nurturing innovation does not always have to begin with an original idea. It is always good to revisit the past, look at what has been done before, what has failed and why and look at ways to fix previous failures to get it right. Some ideas are just ahead of their time and very few ideas are truly original.

I was always very up front with the fact that I considered failure to be part of the innovation process and it was ok for my team to fail. It is important to give people time to experiment and think creatively and most of all to follow their passion. I would give my team members a certain number of days per quarter to pursue something that they were passionate about.

It is also very important to reward creative thinking with an official recognition program and to get outside the office as a team. We would go on excursions to New York, and spend the day with creative people from other agencies. We would also invite outsiders in to participate in innovation sessions or to help solve a problem. This allowed us to cross-pollinate different disciplines from both inside and outside the company for the best possible results.

When you have your team really concentrate, it is possible for them to uncover deep insights and to uncover unmet consumer or professional needs. It is important to understand your consumers and core target markets, so spend the money on research, it will be well worth it. This was a core J&J principle, find a deep insight and then go after it.

Other things that I found to be most beneficial to creating an atmosphere of innovation was encouraging continuous learning, using the 10 types of innovation model to encourage thinking beyond the conventional. Doblin's 10 types often help provide a framework. https://www.doblin.com/ten-types

I specifically encouraged my team to take their ideas to at least five other people and get them to help make it better, to do a mash-up of ideas and innovations from other industries and crowdsource whenever possible. Test everything quickly and inexpensively, beg, borrow and steal shamelessly where it makes sense,

Who mentored you regarding innovation and what did they do to cultivate "big thinking"?

Paul Michaels and Doug Hall are my innovation heroes. They are both very balanced in that they are equal parts Right Brain and Left Brain. Right Brain: they always encouraged creative thinking and bigger thinking and they turn things on their heads. They are also Left Brain in that they have a clear/defined process for innovation. They both always advised us to "Fail Fast, Fail Cheap"

Could you share an example of how you were able to create breakthrough innovation?

You have to think about what you can do versus can't do. When McNeil Labs, a division of J&J, was experiencing recalls and unable to develop future innovation, the team needed to think about innovation in a non-traditional way.

Instead of product innovation in the traditional sense, we thought about other ways to add value for consumers. We developed My Coach for Arthritis and Sleep accessed via 2D codes. These programs were on-line coaching modules to help consumers change lifestyle/behavior – to stay active for less pain, and to optimize routines, and reduce stress for better sleep. Innovation isn't always new products, it's new ways of thinking.

Jeff Sternstein

EVP, Director of Client Services Havas, Digital Innovation, Healthcare

A senior leader at Nestle sent me to Jeff because Jeff had been one of his most influential innovation mentors. He quoted Jeff and said "you have to talk to him", so I did.

How would you define innovation?

I think innovation can truly range from small to large; it's not a matter of size but the idea of looking at something that exists and doing it a lot better.

Who have you seen do innovation well?

Many companies in E-connected health is creating new ways of serving patient needs and dealing with patients tracking themselves.

Technologically addressing the human experience, how to connect people to brand experience and how to offer a blend of services and products that generate value – this is the future of digital health. Digital health is the future of health care so we have to innovate here.

Examples of breakthrough innovation which you've led or of which you've been a part:

I worked on world's first inhaled insulin –something that was truly breakthrough, Exubera®, from Pfizer. I then worked on the world's second inhaled insulin. Brands weren't doing well and there was pressure on us as an agency and lots tension. It was a differentiated product for sure – but was it an innovation? The idea of inhaling insulin vs. injecting was big yet there were flaws. The container wasn't designed to be seen and so it was indiscreet. Sanofi offered inhaled insulin with a handheld version, more discreet but still didn't gain traction. Innovation has to incorporate both a real insight and an idea that solves the problem.

Any words of wisdom in your experience?

Don't get hung up waiting for something to be fully baked, you can bring me the mushy muffins. I didn't want teams to get held up waiting for perfection of an idea. He wanted them to push out the ideas, as this helps people get unstuck and feel confident even if not quite ready. Keep the ideas flowing and allow team members to share even if they are sharing mushy muffin'. Always keep in mind that it is impossible to innovate in a vacuum, and always look up and around, don't just look at the path in front of you.

Ben Wiegand

Global Head, World Without Disease Accelerator, at Janssen Research & Development, LLC

I have had the pleasure of following Ben in many of his innovation adventures. First at J&J Consumer and later working cross-sector in the OTC field, we had the pleasure of working with him. His team was always inspired and passionate.

Now, as he heads a World Without Disease initiative, I have no doubt he can find creative and breakthrough ways to get there – empowering his team with resources and support the way he always has.

How do you define Innovation?

Innovation is an insight that's put into practice (scientific or commercial). It is not just a discovery, it can come from processes, products, solutions – and an idea does not become an innovation until it's put into practice (e.g. iphone in a box is not true innovation) and delivers against a real unmet consumer need.

How do you inspire innovation?

One of my mentors was Neal Matheson. He taught me the value of diversity of team members, the need for a culture that respects that diversity and the importance of always having their backs.   In order for each team member to feel safe and have the ideas flow at top capacity, they have to be given the freedom to operate, and the team MUST get the credit for any innovation. A leader's job is to make it safe for them to fail – just encourage them to fail fast and get on with it.

People can be taught how to innovate and they can be taught how to mentor for innovation. There also needs to be the right mix of ingredients of types of team members, processes, rewards, and nurturing – everything cannot be graded on an 'A' or 'F' scale. There needs to be small wins in between the big ones and they have to be recognized. The team leader must share in the risks and the rewards and there needs to be a blend of insights from outside and inside the organization.

The vision needs to be big, so that there is a win-win for everyone, so people will check their egos at the door.

Who mentored you regarding innovation and what did they do to cultivate "big thinking"?

Neal Matheson was a mentor – he gave us difficult problems to solve. He checked in on progress and he saw the need for a sense of urgency. He encouraged us to think big and take risks – some innovations could take 5-7 years. You need to be thinking about it everywhere, in the shower or car or wherever and be somewhat all-consumed. Solving the problem has to become your passion. He would set up competitive challenges and teams so someone could win. He felt that you needed to have an edge so you did not become complacent.

Could you share an example of how you were able to create breakthrough innovation?

I was part of the rethinking about the BandAid® brand adhesive bandage – We had to evolve and we changed the whole thing with flexible products and stickier adhesives – better wound healing, better comfort.

What advice would you give on how best to inspire innovation?

Always think the best of others, and make sure the team feels like everyone else has something to bring to the table. Respect it if they go outside swim lanes, leave egos at the door, always remember your mission/purpose, and if one team member is successful, everyone is successful.

Neal Matheson

Former head of R&D at Procter & Gamble, J & J and Unilever

When I started my career at P&G, Neal was heading up R&D in beauty. When I managed brands at Johnson & Johnson, he headed up R&D and he used to scare me because he would not allow his team to work on my project unless I was on my game. I had to truly prove the need, that we'd uncovered an insight, or he wouldn't allocate resources. Scary but smart. Neal was and is a strong promoter of the R&D and Marketing partnership as a way to accelerate success. In later years, when I was consulting for J&J, I was a lot more confident in dealing with him, mostly because I was more confident in bringing real unmet needs and insights to the R&D teams he was guiding. He now consults for various pharmaceutical companies and has invited Luminations to work on various projects, to be the voice of the consumer.

How would you define innovation?

When people use it like a buzzword it doesn't mean much. True innovation needs to be something new that actually delivers dollars and adds value. We talk a lot about innovation that isn't really innovation. We need to realize that there are different kinds of innovation.

1) Incremental innovation (80% of company resources) this is a big part of what companies deliver and it needs to happen continuously. This helps us stay ahead of competition, make new claims, hold our place, and is cost-of-entry innovation with a high probability of success. The innovative part is the efficiency of the whole exercise, but these changes add very limited overall value.
2) Disruptive innovation– this type of innovation changes the game. Technology is the foundation but not the disruption. Here you must invent, you've got to figure out how to do better. Focus should be on improving probability of success with a full platform of experiments to find the one that will succeed. Risk is higher but so is reward.
3) Breakthrough innovation – something super significant and often technical. This kind of innovation doesn't just change the game it changes behavior, markets, and habits. It usually involves a technical or scientific breakthrough. It's rare and risky but when it happens it creates tremendous value.

How do you know which type you're aiming for? When people are at their innovative best they are both excited and scared. You need to come together as a team and ask, does it feel really big? Or, to quote Lisa, does it feel really scary?

Inspiring Innovation

How do you nurture innovation and how have you seen others successfully do so?

How I've nurtured innovation is to focus on individual accountability, championing behavior and credibility. All of these allowed me to offer freedom and autonomy. I always make sure people leverage their strengths and that they don't lose track of the fact that there's more than one kind of innovation. It is important to find a way to get access to great people that create a diverse, strong team. Especially if the team is small, they cannot afford a weak link. In addition to freedom, they also need funding. My job was always to provide people, freedom and funding along with checking in to hold the teams accountable.

If you are going to have a great team, they will have weaknesses because they will be quirky and you MUST protect them – I made sure I covered their backs. A leader has to do that because they may not be well-rounded in a traditional sense, so make sure you constitute the team in a way that you cover all bases. Also, teams need to keep in mind that the consumer has to be in the room at all times in order to succeed at innovation.

Who mentored you and how did they do it?

I was mentored by John Goodman, a leading physical chemist in the 1960s. He was brilliant as a scientist and he brought in R&D leaders with a business understanding of business and we called it business-based R&D. He protected us on the technical side but not on the other stuff. He taught me to create great teams. He said to nurture them, protect them and they will deliver for you. He helped me create models for building teams and creating trust within teams. John belittled minutiae as a waste of time and had the guts to tell top management not to sweat the small stuff. I loved the man.

Inspiring Innovation

Examples of breakthrough innovation of which you've been a part:

My favorite example is Hair Care in early days at P&G –the biggest innovation from 1950-1975? I didn't work on it specifically, but the biggest innovation was the hand-held hair dryer, it's a commodity and the net result of them in the mid 60's was that shampooing could became a daily occurrence, where before it was a once or twice a week event. The disruptive innovation was the hand-held blow dryer

I moved the brands at P&G from a weekly shampoo business to a daily hair care business. We created a good conditioner base, not just shampoo. It gave me confidence when my teams delivered great products so I could continue to build and develop. It took me many years. Our R&D was complimented by a great marketing partner, Tom Moore, who saw the value in what we were doing and kept the consumer in the room. Our hair care experience gave us the credibility to guide decisions that led us a large skin care business which ultimately become one of the foundations of beauty care at P&G. The benefit of cross-functional support for innovation was that it got the resources we needed.

I also worked with the person who created the means to launching liquid body washes. The creation of the poof to use with body wash in the shower actually came about in the shower. We wanted to help move the market away from bar soaps to liquid but people wanted lather and a clean rinsed feeling. To get more lather with washes we needed an implement. This innovator was bathing and she built prototypes to use in the shower. She created a hand-made poof and after several tries it delivered the lather and feel she wanted; she called it a stand-up bubble bath. The showers at home and the commute time to work sometimes matter more than working in the office. Don't stop thinking when you walk out the door.

114

Inspiring Innovation

Any words of wisdom for today's innovator?

Transactional learning is core today – you never test your final product, you just test elements and ultimately put it together. You know you are winning if the competition is chasing you. (Note that companies don't always want to accept this.) Diversity, trust and autonomy are paramount for successful innovation. Just like someone always blocks for the quarterback, innovation leaders must always protect their team.

Rick Jentis

Global Category Head, Nestlé

Rick is always reimagining his category, so he is there with the right products when the consumer is ready for them. For example, it used to be food and supplements - today its nutrition. He always saw innovation as the intersection of creativity and leadership. To him, leadership was making sure that the company invested in people and resources and was supportive of the innovation efforts.

What is innovation to you?

At the heart of any great innovation is a creative idea. It would be so much easier if there was a simple formula that would generate brilliant ideas that would guarantee success, but alas, it is not so straightforward. Early in my career I learned three things that helped to increase the likelihood of innovation resonating with the market:

1. **Meet a consumer need.** Every innovation book will tell you that good innovation starts with a deep insight about the consumer. But often times, innovations fail even when the team thought they had a deep insight. When evaluating the idea, it is important to go beyond whether the concept is aligned with the insight, but also is it clear how the product/solution will fit into

the consumer's life, and the bottom line — will they buy it?

2. **Don't compromise on the execution.** Cultivating good innovative ideas into tangible products requires a robust development process. During the development process, teams will encounter obstacles and how they overcome those obstacles will ultimately determine the likelihood of a project succeeding

3. **Cultivate passion for the project.** Many marketers refer to innovations they have launched as their children, considering all the time and effort they pour into them. When marketers have a passion for what they are working on, they want to see it succeed and will seek out multiple solutions for any obstacle that gets in the way. They also have a clearer vision of what it is that will excite the consumer, so they are less willing to compromise on a key element along the way. Cultivating this passion and engagement is where leadership fits into driving successful innovation.

The two most important things I can do is clearly define the expectations for the project, and ensure that the team sees how the project creates value. There is no one right way to lead a team of innovators. In leading teams, I start with the mindset that the people on my team are smart, capable and have a desire for greatness. I then try to cultivate that ability and provide recognition when they are doing a good job.

Anonymous

Former Senior Executive Major Hospital and Healthcare Corporation

I have known this inspiring leader for six years. She changed the game in a major hospital and clinical environment and is now doing the same in corporate America. She leverages her patient understanding and medical background to help improve education for professionals and patients around the globe.

Inspiring Innovation

How would you define innovation?

In a basic sense, innovation is finding new ways of doing things – it's finding solutions. If there's something that is not working well, I will find a new and better way. We don't always talk about innovation, we just talk about getting stuff done.

How do you nurture innovation and how have you seen others successfully do so?

I always tell my team 'Don't wait for perfection or someone else will get there first!' I think it is important to truly believe in your team, just like my parents believed in me. I see it as my job to figure out how to get the resources for my team, and to find creative ways to do more with less.

I encourage my team to always be in performance improvement mode for processes and for themselves. If we believe in what we do, this is the time we need to shine. I believe in what we do and I manage my organization as if it were my very own business, in an intrapreneurial way. I encourage my team to see it as not just a job. We all have ownership and a stake in success. When we innovate, everyone benefits. I also encourage authenticity, the team knows I am being authentic, and this generates trust.

Who mentored you and how did they do it?

My mother was an amazing marketing and creative mind. She owned her own business. She was a respected and admired public speaker and I just saw that as normal. My mom made us imagine things.

When I mentor people, I tell them "you're in an obstacle course, you don't need to jump 100 meters above it, just get over it and on to the next thing." There will be flaws, but that's how you learn. I don't believe in perfection, but I do believe in excellence.

Any words of wisdom in your experience?

I enjoy doing what I do. My words of wisdom are to find a way to focus on what you like to do and then show that passion to other people – that is one important way to inspire innovation.

Anonymous

Head of innovation and new product development at a large laundry and household cleaning consumer goods company

This person worked with me as an R&D partner and went on to be R&D project head. One of the things I always admired is that she had several kids and she made them a clear priority, but still always made the business grow. This was an inspiration to me, and it showed that you don't have to give up your life for your work and vice versa - you can still have big ideas and big successes. Not an easy balance to create, but it can be done.

How do you nurture innovation in your organization?

I nurture innovation by creating an open and trusting environment, where people are truly allowed to brainstorm, building on each other's ideas – all within the context of day-to-day interactions. There are no judgments - just a strong desire to understand the consumer better, meet his/her needs, and drive growth for the company.

Who mentored you regarding innovation and how did they cultivate "big thinking"?

In my past there was not one person who mentored me in innovation – I think it must come from within, from a genuine love of what we do.

What advice would you give on how best to innovate and inspire innovation?

Trends are our friends, so start with this external view. Marry trends to internal strategic views, including: innovation spaces of interest, areas where we need innovation to satisfy trade requirements, internal growth priorities, organizational capabilities, and more. Get out of the office regularly to visit with your consumers and learn. Keep your mind fresh and stimulated.

Marc Greenberger

Managing Partner of Market Performance Group

I originally met Marc when I was very junior in marketing. He was always kind and supportive. He now runs a company that is very innovative in the way it reaches the retail trade. His background was originally operations. He operationalizes innovation like nobody I have ever seen. Marc is always envisioning what the future will look like and what his clients need to succeed in the future. He is the true definition of empathizing and knows his customers intuitively. Marc doesn't wait for the market to be ready, he pre-empts others and gets in there first.

How would you define innovation?

I think innovation should be simple – marketing 101 defines it as an unmet consumer need or an under-met consumer need. This creates an opportunity for innovation. Innovation is a blend of analytical and creative. Guardrails are key and so is trust. Trust means you can fail 49 times but you aren't worried about losing your job so that the 50th time you will succeed.

Innovation doesn't tend to work well in a command and control environment. The traditional hierarchical structure typically slows down the process and doesn't produce great results. Some of the private equity companies do innovation better than larger companies because they work fast, with fewer bureaucratic barriers for quicker implementation. Speed matters.

How do you nurture innovation?

I tell people what needs to be done, not how to do it. Personally, I'm brutally honest and that can be harsh, but it's just my opinion and others know they can disagree. In our company, we value debating candidly and deciding cohesively. The faster you can get to decision points, the better. I try to be soft on people yet hard on results. If you aren't failing, you aren't pushing the envelope enough. Make it okay to make a mistake. It is not alright to make the same mistake twice – you must learn from it.

I ask for an all-in commitment. Integrity and ethics are fundamental. Identify critical hurdles before engaging. Don't think about competition because if you're really innovative, there's room for everyone. Don't spend time thinking about failure, only the possibilities of success. Don't procrastinate. Don't sit at the lunch table waiting for a eureka moment. Innovative leaders must provoke, encourage and motivate their organization. Don't accept no if you believe in your proposition – no is sometimes the beginning of yes.

Who mentored you regarding innovation and how did they cultivate "big thinking"?

I learned the most from peers, not managers. They had capabilities, credentials and qualities that I respected, and they were intelligent people who were humble. Some of the biggest innovators get fired or kicked out of collegiate environments or corporate bureaucracies and go on to do great things.

Examples of breakthrough innovation you've led or which you've been a part?

We wanted to get into Ecommerce. In February of 2017, we put a small team on this project and asked a senior executive to lead this initiative. The team identified the right partner. In March we met at Expo West and put together a deal in a two-hour meeting. On the way home, we devised a three-page launch plan which covered everything from communication to commercialization. Then we got our team together and agreed to go get this done. In April we started business development with a kick-off at a trade show. Six months later we are approaching $1B in Ecommerce business that we are managing. Additionally, we have a runway to get us 3-5 times that business in the next 12-18 months .

Any words of wisdom?

Keep your approach aspirational.

Find the best people you possibly can for the task at hand. Surround yourself with people who are smarter than you. Do not let their great talent and intellect intimidate you. Embrace it!

Make sure you are passionate, have a clear vision and share it.

Anonymous

Former head of Innovation at one of the largest American personal care companies

This person headed up innovation at a large consumer packaged goods company and drove exceptional growth. He developed the company's first real innovation process and created a safe space for his team to innovate on a large scale. He sees innovation as a process applied to creativity and it takes process to generate great ideas - they don't just come out of thin air.

How do you nurture innovation in your organization?

That is a huge question. I think it takes an entire organization, and not just a person to nurture innovation. You can have people that champion getting companies positioned to do innovation well, but it takes an entire leadership team sending consistent signals over time to make it happen. This team must show, consistently, that they

value innovation, that it's financially worthwhile and keep showing the commitment.

You will have some calamitous and hilarious failures, although that should not be the predominant goal. Nobody should feel in jeopardy, but the innovation should not jeopardize the company. It starts at the top, or close to the top, to communicate that innovation is worthwhile, then you can build an organization where people feel safe and they are willing to take risks. People want to challenge themselves and learn – you need to have a balance between joy and fun and the difficulty of creating new ideas that can be executed.

A team leader needs to act as a cheerleader for the department to explain what we are doing and why and how our pipeline could look. This cheerleader must 1) create and support the structure to keep management engaged and 2) proselytize within company 3) challenge the team to keep doing better and better, not to accept the status quo.

I considered myself the blocker. If there was success, success went to the team and if there was a failure I took the hit.

Who mentored you regarding innovation and what did they do to cultivate "big thinking"?

A champion at a high level said we'd take half of all profits and reinvest it in innovation and he did. People, money, organizational alignment helped us deliver. We got a 10:1 return on our investment even with lots of failure. He supported it and loved talking about it to Wall Street and we couldn't get better mentoring and support than this.

A head of R&D taught me how to view innovation as a corporate initiative. He shared how we spent R&D money to get us to lead across the enterprise. He taught me what it was to work on open innovation. He helped us begin with a SWAT team who could do quick technical and consumer assessments and helped us use skunkworks and work cross-functionally with no silos. We got a lot done when there were no silos.

How were you able to bring breakthrough innovation to your current or a past company?

Six years ago, someone on my team had an insight that didn't seem like it made sense. Here is an example of someone who really believed in something so strongly she'd challenge management's beliefs. Despite our arguments, she convinced us to explore different options. The lesson we took away was don't narrow down to an "or" too early, keep your options open. Also tenacity around the consumer brought us to our biggest ideas. She made the difference between a $25MM idea and what ultimately became a $100MM idea.

I believe that the single most important strength you need in innovation isn't creativity, it's the ability to deal with ambiguity. If you do this well, you reach for the biggest ideas. When the bad news comes, have something else ready to go. This helps maintain management support and funding. You ,ay need something a little less shiny until you get to the biggest ideas.

What advice would you give about how best to innovate and inspire innovation?

These are some of my best practices in innovation for existing corporations:

1. **Make sure everyone understands what % of the business** needs to come from innovation, communicate and resource this so they can deliver.

2. **Not every business unit should have the same innovation or growth goals or cadence.** The targets needs to vary by business unit/brand/role in portfolio. Don't deploy resources the same in all situations.
3. **Make clear strategic choices** around which brands or businesses receive strategic resources with a rigorous process.
4. **Allocate financial resources for innovation** – Pay salaries for a team of dedicated marketers and scientists, create a real research budget and invest liberally.
5. **Manage risk proactively** – Agree up front on level of risk the company will take and how much senior management is involved at which stage. Stick to these guardrails.
6. **Create a clear Innovation team structure** – Aligned yet autonomous from brand management. If not autonomous you often sacrifice the future. Make sure innovation is not a marketing training ground but a stretch opportunity assignment.
7. **Ongoing training is critical** – Teach everyone to share the same language of innovation, include cross functional partners. Develop the team as you develop the business. Get out of the office to enrich yourself-- everybody should attend an industry conference outside their category and share with rest of team.
8. **Don't scrimp on Insight Development capabilities** – Job #1 is to translate insights into relevant business opportunities. Be sure to build this expertise. Team members need a deep familiarity with wide array of research techniques, in depth consumer work, concept testing and business model innovation.

Inspiring Innovation Themes

There were so many enlightening and beneficial interviews, I couldn't fit them all into this book. I plan to keep adding to this arsenal of incredibly rich advice on inspiring a culture of continuous innovation. The themes that emerged so far, and that we are nurturing today in our organizations, are just the beginning:

- Teams filled with those who have a passion for innovation, intellectual curiosity and diversity of skills
- A willingness and support to get out of the office and the traditional environment to learn continuously and satisfy deep curiosity A commitment to keep the consumer at the table
- An open invitation to ideate surrounded by a defined process – a blend of discipline and chaos
- A belief that mushy muffins, not yet fully baked ideas and prototypes, need to move forward so we continue to accelerate the pace of innovation – no waiting for perfection
- Mentorship and leadership with a clear and compelling vision and a mission to protect and nurture the team... to always have the teams' backs
- An environment that makes it fun to brainstorm, easy to collaborate, and safe to fail

Part of the magic of continuous innovation is continuous learning and I am always eager to learn more. So please let me know what you learn as you are mentored, mentor others, inspire, ideate, and create the magic of innovation.

Inspiring Innovation

Inspiring Innovation

The Dance of Chaos and Discipline. This is essential for innovation to happen. Bring discipline to the chaos, but don't be afraid of chaos! All ideas have value and ideas come in all sizes.

Environment is important. However, it doesn't always mean fancy furniture. It also means getting out of the office and the traditional environment.

Continuous Learning and Passion. These elements are essential Ingredients for continued innovation.

Mentors Make the Magic Happen. Mentors and leaders need to have a clear and compelling vision and a mission to protect and nurture the team... to always have the teams' backs.

Don't Wait for Perfection to Launch. It is ok to get the ball rolling by sending out 'mushy muffins'.

Make it Safe to Fail and Fail Fast. Create an environment that makes it fun to brainstorm, easy to collaborate, and safe to fail.

Don't Lose Sight of the Audience. The customer is the whole reason innovation is needed and they always need to be at the table.

Grow a Diversified Team. Inspire curiosity, always protect and support them and knock down the fences and roadblocks.

Keep Technology in its Place. While technology is a great tool for innovation, make sure it does not get in the way.

References

References:

Chapter One - A Brief History of Innovation

https://www.theatlantic.com/business/archive/2013/06/innovation-the-history-of-a-buzzword/277067/

http://startupguide.com/tag/history-of-innovation/

https://www.goodreads.com/book/show/18770061-the-cave-and-the-light

http://www.fahrenheit-212.com/a-short-history-of-innovation/

Chapter Two - Innovation – A fine blend of chaos and discipline

The Chaos Imperative: How Chance and Disruption Increase Innovation, Effectiveness, and Success
https://www.fastcompany.com/3021956/googles-nine-principles-of-innovation

https://hbr.org/1985/05/managing-innovation-controlled-chaos

https://www.forbes.com/sites/ekaterinawalter/2013/11/05/the-chaos-imperative-how-provocation-breeds-innovation/#3fc5762287c2

https://www.forbes.com/sites/danschawbel/2013/08/01/ori-brafman-how-chaos-can-benefit-your-workplace/#78a5ec204671

https://www.fastcompany.com/3040223/when-it-clicks-it-clicks

Chapter Three – Environmental Elements

http://www.emeraldinsight.com/doi/abs/10.1108/JKM-04-2013-0136

http://www.thisisinsider.com/coolest-perks-of-working-at-google-in-2017-2017-7#perhaps-one-of-googles-most-well-known-perks-employees-can-eat-every-meal-at-work-for-free-and-save-a-ton-of-money-1

Chapter Four – Mentorship Matters

http://innovationexcellence.com/blog/2013/02/03/midnight-lunch-how-thomas-edison-collaborated/

Chapter Five – Trends and the Power of Associative Logic

https://www.forbes.com/2010/09/15/papadellis-ocean-spray-leadership-managing-interview.html

https://en.wikipedia.org/wiki/Kraft_Dinner

https://www.thedailymeal.com/eat/10-things-you-didnt-know-about-kraft-macaroni-cheese

Chapter Six – Brainstorming for Innovation

https://www.fastcompany.com/3061059/how-to-brainstorm-like-a-googler

Chapter Seven – The Pros and Cons of Technology in Innovation

https://www.brainyquote.com/quotes/quotes/m/mitchellka163583.html

http://bigthink.com/wikimind/the-social-downside-to-the-conveniences-of-technology

http://www.nydailynews.com/life-style/eats/smartphones-blame-slow-service-restaurants-article-1.1879081

Chapter Eight – Magical Thoughts on Innovation from Industry Leaders

http://under30ceo.com/mentorship-is-vital-to-driving-innovation/